Storage Made Easy

Storage
Made
Easy

**Great Ideas for Organizing
Every Room in Your Home**

C A N D A C E   O R D   M A N R O E

Doubleday Book & Music Clubs, Inc.
Garden City, New York

Published by GuildAmerica® Books, an imprint and a registered trademark of Doubleday Book & Music Clubs, Inc., Dept. GB, 401 Franklin Avenue, Garden City, New York 11530

A GUILDAMERICA® BOOKS/FRIEDMAN GROUP BOOK

© 1995 Michael Friedman Publishing Group, Inc.

ISBN 1-56865-128-7

STORAGE MADE EASY
Great Ideas for Organizing Every Room in Your Home
was prepared and produced by
Michael Friedman Publishing Group, Inc.
15 West 26th Street
New York, New York 10010

Project Editor: Elizabeth Viscott Sullivan
Editor: Dana Rosen
Art Director: Jeff Batzli
Designer: Andrea Karman
Layout: Terry Peterson
Photography Editor: Jennifer Crowe McMichael

Color separations by Fine Arts Repro House Co., Ltd.
Printed in Hong Kong and bound in China by Midas Printing Limited

To Meaghan and Drew, as always

C o n t e n t s

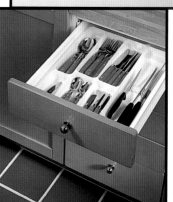

ONE

Taking Inventory

Have you ever had a pair of drop-dead shoes? One with just the right color, baby-soft leather, and a design that keeps the eye coming back for more and always wins a smile? But amid all the perfection, there's one small problem: these favorite shoes are sheer misery on the feet, and all but impossible to wear without some seriously hobbling side effects.

Living in a dream house without proper storage provisions is akin to wearing a pair of ill-fitting, albeit wonderful, shoes. No matter how ideal the home's aesthetic, if it does not address storage needs adequately and efficiently, it just doesn't work.

Home owners always appreciate the convenience of well-conceived storage spaces. But in the rarefied world of design, the idea of storage as an essential feature of a home's success is a radical departure in thinking, one that threatens to redefine interior design as we know it. As we approach the twenty-first century, storage is slowly achieving the status of a fully accredited design issue. Like color, pattern, balance, texture, and traffic flow, storage is increasingly regarded as one of the significant design elements to be considered in planning a room.

To prove just how recently storage has emerged as a design concern, think about how your favorite decorating magazine looked just a year or two ago. Chances are, most of the rooms shown in the photographs were picture-perfect yet totally unbelievable, out of touch with the way most of us really live. In the sumptuous entry hall and family-room photos of a winter issue, where were the mittens, muddy boots, winter coats, and scarves stashed for easy access? What about videocassettes, CDs, and audiotapes? Computer games and other diskettes? Surely they are not all behind closed doors. And what about important papers? Mail? Favorite catalogs and magazines? How about stereo components—or any kind of home electronics? Where, in those delectable rooms, were the notepads and pencils and assorted telephone directories kept? Where, in fact, were the phones?

Not so long ago, addressing storage needs for the everyday items we all have and use in our homes was ignored in interior design. Concern for where to put things was relegated to the plebeian domain of function and thus was conveniently dismissed in the glitzy, would-be aristocratic dream-home books from which many of us gleaned our decorating ideas. (And there are still some heel-draggers in the publication industry today that are reluctant to show something as

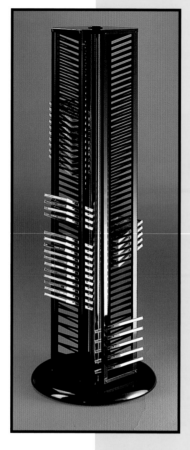

One of the first things an inventory of your home will reveal is your special interests—those hobbies and pastimes that fill your hours. Then, storage of products related to those interests can follow. As strange as it may sound, many music lovers (who perhaps haven't identified themselves as such) lack adequate storage for their recordings. A home inventory quickly exposes the oversight, which can be solved simply by acquiring a space-saving vertical CD tower.

Every household receives mail, pays bills, and relays phone messages. Identify those activities and the materials involved in their pursuit and then streamline these undertakings and their storage with one efficient wall-mounted organizer.

utilitarian as storage shelves for paperwork or a CD rack for a collection of favorite music.)

But while some purist designers and the journalists who write about them cling to the old notion of form as design's sole formal concern, with little regard for function, other industry professionals are paving the way toward greater ease and comfort in the home for all of us. Storage, they acknowledge, is not a luxury but a necessity in creating a truly comfortable living space. In designing a home that is a real haven, ensuring the sufficient storage of belongings is vital.

"I call it 'real-life decorating,'" says New York designer Lyn Peterson of Motif Designs. "Decorating was pretend in the eighties. Now we're secure enough to furnish our homes with things that are our own personal biography. We [in shelter-magazine photographs] are not afraid to show the reading lamps, the bag being returned to Bloomingdale's, the kids' school

Because of the many tasks performed in it, the kitchen requires greater organization and efficiency than any other room in the home. The plethora of cooking utensils, dinnerware, and comestibles that stock this room demands careful preplanning if the space is to function efficiently, look good, and reveal minimal clutter.

knapsacks, the TVs. We want real-life solutions. Where *do* the mounds of mittens go in winter? We no longer want homes as shrines to decorating, but as answers to how we live."

San Francisco designer Agnes Bourne goes a step further. She is convinced that interior design is a healing art, not just an aesthetic sensibility. Finding inventive storage solutions is one of the most therapeutic treatments this healing art has to offer. "Comfort has a lot to do with design as a healing art because it takes the aggravation out of your world. It starts by organizing your home to support what you do," explains Bourne.

To design for comfort, Bourne recommends making a list of what makes you uncomfortable. "If you can't find your tax records or things in your kitchen or bath, find better storage solutions so these functions no longer require a lot of time and energy. It's like putting your underwear on backwards everyday. It's a needless aggravation," she says.

By taking a careful inventory of your home, you can remove much of the irritation from your daily life. When storage needs are finally addressed in an efficient, easy-to-manage fashion, life becomes much simpler and home is transformed into what we always knew it could be: our safe retreat from the pressures of the world outside. Without the frantic scramble to find things, or the taxing stretch to reach them, our lives are calmer. We're ready to face the day without unnecessary nuisance and hindrance. With orderly storage, our home becomes a supportive extension of ourselves instead of another adversary. Everything we want and need is within reach, intelligently stored for our ease.

Questions Before Answers

Once your list of storage needs is organized according to rooms and prioritized according to need, it's time to investigate some of the possible storage options. There are many choices, which will be more closely examined in the following chapters. But in finishing your inventory, the general types of storage solutions should be addressed, with specific configurations to be determined later.

Some of the questions to ask yourself in deciding on an overall approach are: can storage requirements be met within the existing major living spaces, or do separate storage rooms need to be created? Can storage be provided through furnishings—existing or new purchases—or are architectural built-in features needed? Which rooms are in need of innovative storage designs and which can benefit from a simple, ready-made stacked-shelving system? Would open, exposed storage be more desirable than hidden, behind-closed-doors storage? What is the overall decorating style of the home, and which storage alternatives lend themselves best to that style? What about the scale of the materials to be stored?

Solutions vary greatly, according to the amount of space needed. Once these questions have been answered, you're ready to begin tailoring storage solutions to meet your needs.

Getting Started

 Step 1 **Room by room, take a walking tour of your home,** notepad and pen in hand. In each room of your house, jot down the situations that make you uncomfortable (e.g., the extra roll of toilet tissue is never where you need it when you need it; or, dressing requires twice as much time as it should because belts are stashed in the back of a drawer that has to be virtually emptied of all contents in order to see them). For the most comprehensive list, run through an imaginary day, envisioning all activities that are typically pursued in each room.

With the simple addition of a few pegs for storing outerwear and a sturdy bench, this entryway is instantly transformed into a mud room. The bench not only functions as a place to sit and comfortably remove footwear, but serves two storage needs, too: it provides a surface for leaving bags and schoolbooks as well as a spot to tuck away storm boots.

Taking a mental walk through your daily home routine is the best way to reveal your storage criteria. Beginning at the front door, storage needs are immediately illuminated: the home requires a tidy depository for the hanging of coats, hats, handbags, mittens, and other items that need to be taken or worn to and from school and work. Objects that are called on less frequently can be stored in more permanent ways—within stacked boxes or deep in trunks.

Step 2 **Be honest with yourself!** If you enjoy giving yourself a pampering pedicure on your living room sofa during late-night TV programs, admit it. Your pedicure accoutrements need to be stored in a nearby location to be convenient. Remember: nobody can tell you how to use your home; nor can anyone tell you what's important to have stored close at hand. Your needs are legitimate for one reason and one reason only: they are yours. Let your home express who you are.

Step 3 After mentally playing out a day, go back and imagine how, if you were granted a wish list, you might **utilize your rooms in ways in which they are not currently used.** (For example, perhaps you've always wanted the guest bedroom to be a sewing room—or a little home theater.) What would your storage needs be if you gave a second life to these spaces? When you're ready to make decisions on storage, don't disregard these dream rooms. Planning for them is a sure way to start realizing them more quickly than you thought.

Step 4 **Give yourself enough time to get organized.** Identifying and correcting all your storage needs probably won't happen overnight. So get organized about getting organized. Go back over your list of storage problems and highlight those that bother you the most. These are the ones to rectify first.

Step 5 After setting your priorities, **pick the room that offers the greatest storage challenge**. Start your reorganizing by concentrating your energies in that room.

In Plain Sight

Storage doesn't have to mean hidden from sight within the dark confines of drawers, cabinets, or closets. Instead, storage can mean a designated place of containment that's well within view—even on proud display.

In fact, storage containers themselves can be objets d'art or room accessories that are decorative in their own right. Handwoven baskets or a collection of interesting boxes which ornament a room and add to its ambience make excellent receptacles for smaller items in need of a home. Use your creativity in displaying these containers, perhaps looking to the wall as well as a tabletop.

Also, don't be confined in your thinking of what requires storage. Sure, papers and notepads qualify as objects to be stored away—but so do colorful heaps of ruby red apples.

Step 6 **Break down the problem areas into manageable units.** You have your list of top-priority storage problems. But some of them may seem overwhelming (nothing in the living room is handy, for example). Rather than becoming intimidated by the huge task looming before you, get specific. Determine what isn't handy. Maybe it's the TV, VCR, and stereo remote control devices—they're never where you can find them. Make a specific notation identifying that problem on your list. Then move on to the next situation in the room. Maybe favorite magazines are scattered hither and yon, when you'd really like them in one central place. Make a note. Don't despair if your list gets a bit lengthy. The more data you collect, the easier working out the solutions will be. Remember, nobody's home has perfect storage alternatives; a family's needs and activities are constantly changing, so their storage solutions must evolve as well.

Step 7 Before attempting to find storage solutions to the top-priority problems in a room, consider another option. **Don't be afraid to unclutter by removal.** Toss things into the trash (recycling whenever possible), or box items for a garage sale or for pickup by a favorite charitable organization. Not everything we cling to in our homes is essential. Much is simply "stuff," with an unfortunate habit of following us, home to home, with magnetic attraction. Have an ample supply of bags, boxes, or trash bags handy when taking inventory—and use them. The papers you wrote for graduate school may have seemed like treasures in the seventies or eighties, but maybe they aren't critical to your family's development at this stage of your life. Maybe the storage space they take

Taking inventory of your wardrobe is a prerequisite for making sense of a closet with a well-planned storage concept. Shoe lovers will require a different closet-storage configuration from a clotheshorse whose weakness is woolen sweaters.

up could be better utilized by housing a less dispensable item—like your child's school supplies.

Step 8 To aid in determining whether to toss or save, **apply this simple test:** have you used the items in question over the past year? The past two years? If you haven't referred to items in that length of time (unless they're something in a sacrosanct category of their own, such as federal tax records), it's a safe rule of thumb to assume these items are not essential to your daily life. Remove them—unless they have possible vintage value or personal significance.

Step 9 If some of these seldom-if-ever-used items (especially dining- or kitchenware) are hand-me-downs from grandmother, **have an expert or a friend versed in antiques take a look** before relegating the possessions to the trash heap—and forever regretting your rashness. Often, the most unlikely pieces (or those most unpleasing to your eye) are collectibles. But aside from possible monetary value, also think through the sentimental meaning of items before disposing of them: is it possible that an item with no meaning for you might be of some value to your children or their children? Hanging on to trash is a crime, but throwing away heirlooms is even worse. Proceed thoughtfully.

Step 10 Look over your list of storage needs and **create sets of similar objects.** Chances are, related items exist (for example, paper goods or linens of various

Like with Like

No matter what the room, no matter what the furnishing, cabinet, or closet, one rule simplifies storage: group similar items together.

A bedroom closet, in particular, illustrates the wisdom of this organizational tip. Within this limited space, the arrangement of stored items according to related groupings greatly maximizes available space. Hanging shirts together means a precise vertical space is all that's necessary to accommodate them. Ties arranged on the back of the door provide quick retrieval, but just as important, this organized grouping efficiently utilizes what could be dead space.

types). For the most logical storage solutions, group similar items together for consideration as storage mates. In the long run, such groupings will help to conserve precious space and also spark a logical connection in your memory, which will enable quick retrieval.

Step 11 Even though some items to be stored may not look similar (shoes, for instance, would seem to demand a different storage treatment than coats), it often makes sense to **store items with a similar function together.** Thus, make a set or group of items with a related function: outdoor wraps—hats, scarves, coats, mittens, and even shoes—may be creatively stored together in one area, with one special storage device.

Step 12 On your inventory list, think about **grouping items of similar shape and size.** Belts, ties, and scarves all have a long, narrow shape—and that may influence your storage options and conserve space.

Step 13 Not everything in a disturbingly cluttered room is necessarily an object better hidden than exposed. When poorly organized, even prize collectibles can create a sense of chaos. In taking inventory, **don't forget about collectibles.** Chances are, there is a better solution to displaying them—one that is more orderly and streamlined, tidying the overall look of the room. Make note of collectibles that appear even slightly disorganized; then work later at finding a better display/storage system.

A child's bedroom can be a storage nightmare due to the chaotic assemblage of toys and clothing housed therein. But a few affordable, easy-to-install devices, such as plastic-coated wire shelving and stackable plastic cubes, make cubbyholing a logical solution.

Persevere, Persevere

Just thinking about all the preliminary effort in figuring out workable storage solutions for your home may seem overwhelming. You may feel that you and your family are out there all alone, with nary a decent storage option, while the rest of the world is neatly and effortlessly tucking their possessions into perfectly provided storage cubbyholes.

But before you become disheartened, rest assured that the more thoroughly and honestly you take inventory of your storage needs, the more easily you will be able to decide upon storage

solutions. In most cases, the right alternatives will practically present themselves, based on the data you gathered as groundwork. And you are not out there alone in the storage hinterlands. The home with adequate storage is rare, indeed. It isn't just apartments, condominiums, duplexes, or smaller single-family homes that have inadequate storage. Even the most palatial mansion has less-than-optimum storage capacity in some of its rooms. Creating attractive and functional storage areas in an existing home is a bit of an uphill battle, to

be sure—but it's some consolation to know that the challenge is common.

Once you've accepted the fact that new storage ideas need to be explored in your home, the fun can begin. Finding the right solutions to your needs is like solving a puzzle, and when all the pieces are finally in place, it's even more rewarding than the most intricate jigsaw. Sometimes, the most pleasure is derived from operating under the tightest constraints: even on a shoestring budget, storage concepts that are innovative in function and high in style can be found.

Opposite: Storage solutions demand recognition of the individual storage space as well as of the individual utilizing that space. This work area is highly personalized, catering to a free spirit who doesn't mind odd items stored within close proximity.

Above: This space, in contrast to the one on the opposite page, points to a mentality more comfortable with a sleek arrangement in which stored objects are better concealed than displayed. The beneath-the-daybed drawers keep objects hidden, while the shelves above the desk organize materials in discrete groups.

TWO

A Storehouse of Options

After you have taken a thorough inventory of your home, determining what works and what doesn't in its storage capacity, you should now have a clear idea of your needs. When all your storage shortcomings are identified, much of your work is done. The remaining job requires focusing and employing a little creativity. From an abundance of options, you must now determine which solutions best solve storage problems for you.

Storage requires not just a generic approach, but one that is designed especially for you and your family or housemates. Even physical factors such as your height play a role in which storage options work best for you. Tall CD towers won't be as satisfactory for a short person as a low-slung horizontal rack configuration would be, for example.

To plan storage intelligently, it's important to know all the options. More storage organizers are available today than ever before. The market is saturated with stackable clear boxes, nesting floral-print boxes, wire and plastic carts, zip-up bags and boxes, sliding baskets, adjustable shelving, drawers, clip-on caddies, and so on. Though a great convenience, the increased options also mean that decision making is much more involved than it was in the past. With so many ready-made products, as well as other options such as built-ins to choose from, knowing your storage needs doesn't mean automatically knowing which

Depending upon your passions, a special room may be in order to accommodate the storage of materials associated with your pastimes. Drying flowers is a prime example. A special work area is every gardener's dream, with storage space for container plants, herbs, and seeds, plus areas to hang flowers to dry.

After identifying your storage needs, take time to familiarize yourself with potential solutions instead of assuming there's only one answer to every problem. If the items are limited in number and worthy of showing off, formal cabinetry may be unnecessary. Here, simple wooden shelves get the job done with style.

China and pottery are among the most colorful collectibles, and it's a shame to hide them behind closed doors. An understanding of storage options can reveal the superiority of an open-shelf cabinetry system for an outstanding collection that deserves to be seen throughout the day, not just at mealtimes.

products or storage solutions will best address those needs. You may not even be aware of some storage merchandise that is new to the market, and there are some do-it-yourself architectural ideas that you may not have considered. In solving storage problems, lack of knowledge can result in dissatisfaction later on. Resist the urge to rush to the nearest retail store in search of armfuls of organizers. Even more dangerous is the urge to mail-order a houseful of products from one of the popular storage-specialty catalogs before you have considered all the options. Decisions made on the basis of only partial information usually end up only partially satisfactory.

Take time to acquaint yourself with all the possible alternatives for solving your storage problems before making any decisions to build or buy. The information in this chapter will acquaint you with a range of options.

Handy Holders

Finding manufactured containers for storing household items is now easier than ever. The products are readily available, and what's more, well-engineered, highly functional containers no longer always mean unsightly appearance and ungainly design. Manufacturers' newly honed eye for aesthetics means that even the most utilitarian box or shelf eschews a thrown-together look, striving instead for more furniturelike styling that blends seamlessly with the rest of the home.

The increased emphasis on appearance has another advantage: offerings are spanning more and more diverse designs and looks. This ensures easy coordination of storage products with the various decorating styles and themes of homes, from the look of timeless traditional to cutting-edge contemporary.

Kitchen work areas foster some of the home's most creative and custom-designed storage solutions, including pullout drawers and panels for caddying everything from bottle openers to cookbooks.

Where to Find Portable Organizers

To conduct your own consumer survey of storage containers, start with mail-order specialty catalogs.

All products in such catalogs pertain to storage, so for a comprehensive overview of what's available, it's hard to find a better source. In addition, some companies specializng in furniture or housewares also offer storage containers appropriate for their product lines. To start the get-acquainted mission, flipping the pages of catalogs in the comfort of your home beats driving from store to store to see the available options.

After perusing catalogs and getting an idea of what's out there in product lines, make a trip to any major department store or discount store to find storage items suitable for your needs.

The kitchen departments in retail stores will have lots of containers and storage items appropriate for culinary tasks. Bath shops, too, are now offering more storage products. Good news to those with shoestring budgets: mass-market stores have a large selection of organizers that can be put to use in nearly any room of the house or worked into intricate configurations for the closet. Even if budget isn't a prime consideration, it makes sense to consider the easy-to-use, cost-conscious solutions available at these stores before embarking on more costly structural changes to the home.

Types of Portable Organizers

One of the most appealing features of portable, ready-made storage containers is their versatility. They come in nearly all materials, shapes, sizes, and looks. The following tips scan the various offerings, suggesting possible uses for each.

One thing to remember about portable storage containers is that they can be made to fit. Because of the variety of sizes of the individual units, the right ones can be found to work in a configuration that conforms to your space limitations. Containers can be organized vertically or horizontally; various sizes of containers can be grouped together in modular fashion in a single, tidy-looking configuration. Because the individual pieces can be small enough to hold many items of the same type, they greatly simplify your life: no more frantic fumbling through a mishmash of belongings in drawers or cabinets. Suddenly, life is

Portable organizers come in all shapes, sizes, and materials. Whether your storage needs are for cocktail napkins or an odds-and-ends assortment of kids' toys, there's a handy solution waiting in catalogs or retail stores.

much easier, with what you need right at your fingertips, organized in a container of its own.

Tip 1 Consider wicker or other sturdily woven baskets as containers. Baskets make excellent receptacles for organizing important papers, magazines, or newspapers to be recycled.

Try small baskets for stashing golf balls or marbles. Or create your own baker's basket to collect an overflow of kitchen tools and utensils. Baskets designed with flat backs for wall mounting make excellent receptacles for lightweight articles such as letters, bills, or wooden spoons. Tall rattan baskets (like the clothes hampers of old) make excellent umbrella stands or holders for sports equipment such as baseball bats, tennis racquets, fishing rods, or even skis and ski poles.

With their rustic good looks and the appearance of handcraftsmanship, baskets add a nice textural touch to any room decor. Storage baskets look more like design-enhancing accessories than simply functional containers—which is precisely the point.

Tip 2 Rediscover the basic box.

Although corrugated cardboard gets the job done while you are moving, it doesn't do much to enhance the look of your home when enlisted as a full-time storage facility. But close cousins to plain cardboard—patterned or solid-color paper boxes—accomplish the same catchall function, with more style. These boxes are available in most stores, including five-and-dimes and some pharmacies, and they are good for hiding clutter from newspaper clip-

Underfoot and on the Wall

There's probably a lot more storage space in your home than you are aware of. Instead of purchasing additional case goods, built-in or portable shelving, cabinetry, or drawers, you may be able to utilize existing space on the walls or floors for organizing household goods.

Consider using pegboard to organize everything from jewelry, hats, coats, and sports equipment (tennis racquets, skis, and golf clubs, for starters) to backpacks, belts, ties and scarves, and even chairs (hung upside down, in the Shaker style).

Space to consider for storage includes areas beneath end tables, cocktail tables, and consoles, which can be attractively organized with colorful mounds of quilts or other vintage textiles, displays of antique tools or large pottery, or neatly stacked books and magazines.

pings to canceled checks. Consider them for their stacking ability—on shelf tops or directly on the floor. Some of the boxes are specially designed to serve as recipe, baseball card, or photograph files, providing a unified, orderly appearance as well as excellent organization.

Quality varies greatly among boxes, which range from lightweight cardboard to more durable substances such as laminated plastic, wood, and metal. Select a box sturdy enough to house your materials over time. A lightweight box may be a fine container for scraps of lace or buttons, but a flimsy box that disintegrates under a too-heavy load creates more stress in the long run than it relieves in the short term.

With all the available boxes on the market, be sure to pick ones of a size and shape compatible with the proposed contents. Letter-size envelopes, for example, should be stored in boxes with an appropriate ($8\frac{1}{2}$ inch [21.5cm]) width.

Even though a box may not be sold with file organizers, you can make these yourself or purchase them if your boxes are of standard size. Choose boxes deep enough to accommodate your desired contents, leaving space at the top for file tabs.

In selecting boxes as organizers, decide whether visibility of contents is an asset or detriment. For items such as audiocassettes, CDs, and videocassettes, a transparent plastic box is desirable, because it will permit quick identification and retrieval of materials. For personal papers or objects that look disorganized even when they are contained in a box, you will probably want to select a patterned or solid-color box.

Even a laundry room can take on a decorated look with a little bit of efficient storage detailing. Wire wall shelves house a tidy display of folded laundry as well as a few eye-catching collectibles included for visual interest.

Tip 3 **Specialize—but be wise.**

When appropriate, select storage units that have been designed to serve a specific function. Special CD columns, for example, make a lot of sense because their shape is based on the dimensions of a CD, and so they won't waste any unnecessary space. Wine racks and cutlery trays are logical choices for the same reason. Sewing boxes, on the other hand, don't necessarily differ significantly from any other kind

of box—except, perhaps, in price, which may be slightly higher. It is a good idea is to look for a generic organizer, which can often be equally effective in getting the job done, before purchasing a specialized storage unit.

Tip 4 **Consider portable drawers as a flexible alternative to fixed case goods or built-in storage areas.**

Drawers are the linchpin of storage. Not only do they constitute the basic unit of case goods and built-in storage,

but they are also available now in portable form, providing a new range of affordable freedom for the owner. When attached to casters and appropriately scaled, affordable laminated particleboard drawers are ideal organizers for under-the-bed clutter. In closets or the bedroom, stackable drawers are wonderful solutions for storing clothing and fashion accessories that need protecting. They cost a fraction of what "real" furniture costs and offer flexibility in terms of placement and configuration that furniture does not. Transparent plastic drawers are especially suited for containing shoes or other items that should be easily seen.

Wire, locker-style drawers or bins are a unique form offering many advantages, the most important being their roomy storage depth. Whereas the standard storage drawer is only several inches deep, the depth of locker-style drawers can be a foot or more, which makes them especially handy in the kitchen to organize tall detergents and bottles of cleaning products. (In the kitchen, locker drawers are often stacked in a rolling utility cart that can easily be pushed out of view into a closet or even topped with a flat laminated surface to serve as a work space.) Other advantages of this type of unit are its light weight and range of colors, from bright primaries to neutrals and pastels.

Old-fashioned wooden trunks have long been valued as repositories for storing out-of-season blankets and clothing.

Tip 5 If it can't be boxed or stashed in a basket or drawer or on a shelf, a storage bag may be the solution.

To store and protect wool sweaters, delicate lingerie, or heavy suits, zip-up plastic storage bags are a space-saving solution. Available in a wide range of sizes and shapes, they can be stacked one atop the other or hung from a clothes hanger or peg in the closet. In the bath, small versions with individual zip-up compartments make superb caddies for storing toiletries.

Plastic, wall-mounted jewelry bags are compartmentalized to ensure efficient storage.

Functional Accessories

Tip 6 Make existing home accessories and objets d'art do double duty as visual decor and storage units.

While baskets and boxes made specifically as storage organizers are readily available on retail shelves or from the pages of a catalog, these certainly aren't the only sources. Accessories you already have in your home—most obviously, decorative baskets and boxes—can be enlisted for the utilitarian function of organizing your household belongings.

Transforming existing pieces into storage obviously saves on precious space. And because the accessories or furnishings were acquired for their aesthetic value, blending them into your home's decor isn't even a consideration—they're already there because they visually work in your decorating scheme. Don't leave a nested set of beautifully crafted Shaker boxes resting empty one atop the other. Fill them with stamps, newspaper clippings, paper clips, or thread—anything small that you need organized and stored.

Baskets and boxes are only a starting point. Other objects that can creatively contain smaller items include large bowls (you'll be amazed at how many odds and ends can be stored in them), glass showcases (these are ideal for collections you want to display, but are also appropriate to house keepsake pieces that aren't necessarily visual—kids' schoolwork, for example), old library card-catalog drawers (great for recipe storage), church offering plates (good resting grounds for jewelry), antique shipping crates (try putting these to

Make your furniture do more than look good and take up space. Attractive pieces, including antiques, can be found that function amazingly well as storage units. A wall of old apothecary drawers can store anything from jewelry to napkin rings while providing space for displaying collectibles.

An armoire or built-in cabinet begs for goods to go within its doors. In a bedroom these can provide the ideal space to store sweaters or other clothes. In a living room, books, files and papers can be neatly tucked inside.

work as bins for recyclables), old pails (for paintbrushes, scissors, and so on), or even reused chicken coops and lobster traps, which make attractive holders for blankets or quilts or children's toys. All that's required is the imagination to envision the storage possibilities of even the most unlikely of accessories or funky collectibles.

A Furnished Cache

Tip 7 In selecting new furniture, be sure to size up more than style. Ask if the amount of storage that the furnishing will offer justifies the amount of space it will occupy.

A twig dresser for sale in an art gallery tempted me with its one-of-a-kind design, which made it look like a strangely contorted woodland creature. Although the dresser was valuable as art,

Dual-Purpose Architectural Elements

Not all built-in storage must be used only for storage. Some of the most innovative storage spaces appear in the most unlikely places—beneath seating, between the walls, behind closed (but not exactly closet) doors.

Examine the beneath-the-seat storage possibilities of banquette sofa seating, built-in breakfast booths, and window seats. Two other storage areas worth looking into are a walled room-divider partition, which can be gridded with shelving, and a solid "wall" of louvered doors, which provides a clean look to a room while containing nearly limitless storage space.

ultimately it had to be passed up. Its minimal number of drawers and small amount of countertop space didn't justify the floor space it would devour—it was over six feet (1.8m) wide.

All furniture is not created equal when it comes to storage capacity. The good news is that there are many case goods available that are as important for their storage function as they are for their form. Home entertainment centers, with their long shelves and capacious cabinets, are intended to store home electronics equipment, books, and collectibles, plus any kind of overflow that's best hidden behind cabinet doors. Other pieces worth investigating are armoires, trunks, sideboards, and nearly any style of cabinets (chimney, corner, Hoosier, or hanging, to name a few). Even the bed can become a functional storage unit when it's designed with headboard and/or footboard shelving, under-the-mattress drawers, and built-in side cabinets or shelving.

Architectural Answers

While freestanding furniture and portable organizers can provide a clean look and an efficient retrieval system, one of the most streamlined solutions to storage remains among the most costly and the most time-consuming to add: architectural built-ins. Not all structural changes have to entail major expense or out-lay of time, however. Among the countless variations of permanent shelving, cabinetry, drawers, cupboards, arched niches, closets, islands, room dividers, and entire closeted walls, there are some affordable options. Open-shelf bookcases and build-it-yourself entertainment centers are among the most cost-efficient architectural solutions, if the lumber of choice is not finely grained but is sufficiently sturdy and best suited for painting.

Stairway to Storage Heaven

Take advantage of the diagonal dead space beneath a staircase or under the eaves by adding a "built-in" storage case with a few boards and nails.

Even the crawl space behind a closet door on a second- or third-floor room can become usable square footage if analyzed with an open mind. The on-the-slant space is perfect, for instance, for accommodating a low-slung futon. Suddenly, guests have their own "room"—thanks to a little ingenuity in finding new solutions to storage.

An additional advantage of exploring spaces under eaves and staircases for storage possibilities is this: when put into active duty as functional storage areas, these spaces acquire a look of importance, becoming more visible as architectural features.

Tip 8 The most cost-efficient architectural storage elements that can be added to a room are those that are applied directly to the wall with minimal wood, without first requiring demolition and reconfiguration of the wall.

In some spaces, there often simply isn't enough room to indulge in building out from the walls with added-on shelving. When creating extra storage is essential, there's an easy option: build recessed storage compartments between the studs.

For easy, built-in recessed shelf space, cut out the plaster or drywall between the studs to the desired shelving dimensions, then build and install shelves to fit the space. Between-the-studs shelves can be finished around the edges with molding for an always-been-there look. The inside of the recessed shelves can be newly painted or papered.

Basements and top floors with sloped ceilings don't have to be dreary, uninhabited dungeons. Its skinny walls lined with uniform and inexpensive shelving, the basement space shown here is transformed into a gallerylike space with its collection of stored housewares.

THREE

Kitchens and Dining Areas

No room in the house faces more demands than the kitchen. As the space where our food is stored, prepared, and cleaned up after dining, the kitchen must provide a variety of different services, all essential to daily life. As home entertaining becomes more and more popular, the kitchen is required to perform all its original functions, only better: more efficiently and more professionally, leaving greater time for socializing between the hosts and guests. And with more stay-at-home "cocooning" taking place among family members, the kitchen once again emerges as the hub of the house, the place not only to prepare food, but to sit down and review the day's events while vegetables are being sautéed and sauces are simmering on the stove.

With cooking reaching state-of-the-art levels among home chefs, more and more couples are enjoying their culinary passions as a team. Lest the activities of too many chefs spoil the soup, storage must be streamlined to a science in the kitchen in order for twosomes to cook efficiently and con-genially together.

With all these functions required of today's kitchen, storage—creative, efficient, and good-looking—isn't a matter of wishful thinking; it's essential. But

This dramatic top-floor loft, adorned with shelving all the way to the exposed beams, serves as a gallery-like repository for pottery and other objets d'art.

talk to any five home owners, and four will tell you that their kitchen still isn't up to par in meeting their storage needs. This is especially true of gadget lovers, who can't resist bread machines, pasta makers, electric crêpe pans, woks, madeleine pans, food processors, coffee bean grinders, juicers, espresso machines, and, of course, coffeemakers. All of these take up valuable space and must somehow be organized and stored.

Thriving culinary businesses don't make it easy for one to resist gadgetry. Even harder to ignore is the temptation to accumulate, almost like collectibles, an array of tableware: a casual set of pottery, another set for alfresco dining, the wedding china, the heirloom set from grandmother, an antique collection too perfect to pass up—and so on, until dinnerware threatens to be your undoing. Finding a sensible, easy-access place to store these favorite dishes, plus their equally numerous counterparts, stemware and flatware, is a task that requires real thought.

If you happen to be among the crowd that manages to eschew the high-dollar gadget purchases but find yourself compulsively drawn to smaller culinary aids—wooden spoons of every size and type known, egg separators, apple corers, ice cream scoopers, corn-cob holders—your storage problems are of a different nature. Often, countertop containers are as far as you need to look to acquire a neat, clean appearance and an organized retrieval system for your kitchen helpers.

Whatever your particular kitchen storage problems, there is ample reason to be optimistic about solving them—without having to go bankrupt in the

Just as every home chef brings his or her personality to the food and table, the kitchen should be just as distinctive. In its arrangement of storage features, the kitchen should cater to the individual needs, habits, and preferences of those who use it. Standard cabinet heights, for example, don't work for all people all of the time. A row of shorter-than-average closed cabinets above a counter may be all that's necessary for storing precious dinnerware too fragile to withstand much heavy stacking. Should you have favorite tableware you would like to see on display, warming and accessorizing the room, then an open shelf configuration above the cabinets to the ceiling may be the prescribed solution.

process. For years, inadequate kitchen storage could only be remedied by remodeling, which was generaly cost-prohibitive. Spending tens of thousands of dollars to make spaces more efficient and bring in a few more shelves and cabinets hardly seemed worth it. But today, a wealth of affordable alternatives utilize existing space better, without requiring any costly structural changes.

Many of the same storage requirements apply to both the kitchen and the dining room, so this chapter will look at storage tips for both areas.

Tip 1 **Clear out unused clutter to make room for the important items that require storage solutions.**

This tip is worth repeating for each room in the house, but it's especially important to apply it in the kitchen. Chipped dishes, mismatched or gas-station glassware, silver-plated olive trays you received as a wedding gift but never use—these pieces need to be removed from your space-limited kitchen or dining room; for that matter, you may want to remove them entirely from your life, which probably has enough clutter of its own. Have a garage sale, if that's your style, or phone a charity to come pick up what you can't use. Try to recycle whatever you can before resorting to the trash.

Tip 2 **For the most efficiency, store items as close as possible to the place they will be used.**

It makes sense to store fine china, table linens, sterling silver, candlesticks, vases, and crystal close to the dining room table, where they will be

Making a Culinary Statement

Just because objects belong to the kitchen doesn't mean they belong behind closed doors. And, just because a few of these objects are functional to the core, recruited into service at each mealtime, doesn't mean they don't also have shapes and forms of real visual interest.

Dig through your kitchen drawers and reappraise your work tools. You may be surprised at how many of them have sculptural qualities that, put in their best light, captivate the eye with their compelling lines. Ferret out a few favorites, then try arranging them in a pleasing fashion. Hung from hooks or nails in a neat row beneath other kitchen collectibles, workaday utensils such as potato mashers and gravy spoons take on a new dimension—one of charm that cozies up the kitchen.

enlisted into service. In the kitchen, storage can be planned around the room's basic functions. Keep oils, spices, and cooking utensils—pots and pans, electric skillets, griddles, and so on—close to the range; keep food storage areas (the refrigerator and pantries/cupboards) close to one another and to your favorite grocery-unloading spot; keep detergents, sponges, dish towels, and cleaners within a swivel-step away from the sink and dishwasher. In addition, be sure to leave space for a wastebasket somewhere near the sink in order to ensure efficient cleanup. And it's important to find a convenient yet hidden location to collect recyclables in organized bins—an environment-conscious measure that's also becoming an essential part of kitchen cleanup in most homes today.

Baker's Dozen

In the kitchen, it's imperative to create storage space even where there is none. To glean ideas, start by analyzing a kitchen plan you admire for its functional streamlining: chances are good the kitchen plan includes a center work/storage island of some sort. Simply translate that idea into a storage solution that works in your existing kitchen.

A baker's rack may be the answer you require. Easily deployed, it can be plopped into the middle or near-middle of the room without having to rely on the safety of a wall to make sense. A striking collection of Fiestaware becomes an arresting visual element when housed in this makeshift island.

Smaller side shelving units can be pushed up to the baker's rack to form a tiered look—and a great storage center.

Shelving

A good starting point for any discussion of kitchen storage is shelving, for there's no way to have a functional kitchen without it. Shelving, in the context of this discussion, doesn't mean only open shelves adhered to the wall, but also those shelves within cabinetry—the keystone of kitchen storage. Proper spacing of shelves within cabinetry and on the walls is essential to a well-organized kitchen. Sometimes, however, even when the configurations of cabinet shelves are acceptable, a mess can occur from trying to cram so many dissimilar items onto the same shelf. Nothing is more frustrating than reaching for the vegetable steamer but first having to take out every pot and pan you own.

But thanks to the great selection of highly specialized organizers that are now on the market, a solution to this problem is only a few dollars and a couple of minutes away.

Spice racks are sometimes best approached with a divide-and-conquer philosophy, made easy by these widely available wire wall-mounted caddies.

Tip 3 **Use shelf dividers to organize wide shelves into narrower compartments, grouping like items for easy access.**

Dividers are a great invention that can take the jumble of your pots and pans and turn it into a neat array of organized cookware: all lids within one divided compartment; all skillets within another; pots in yet another; and food processor, blender, and other same-size gadgets within a convenient, delineated space of their own. You'll be amazed how much more pleasant life can be, thanks to this one simple tool for organization.

Paying attention to how kitchen cabinets and cupboards are internally mapped can help you avoid costly renovation and rebuilding. Fitted wire shelving that slides easily out on gliders can turn a disheveled cabinet interior into the picture of organization.

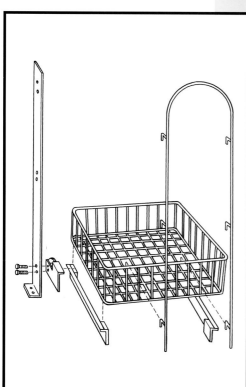

Cabinet Shelves

One of the biggest inefficiencies in any kitchen is the poor spacing of shelves within cabinetry. Standard dimensions too often are installed with no thought to the real needs of the individual. It's impractical to assume that everyone needs, or can put to good use, fourteen inches (35.6cm) or more of height per shelf within a cabinet. Instead, most of us have more specialized needs—for shallow shelves for plates (who wants to deal with the danger of plates stacked too high?); narrow, shallow shelving for bowls; and taller shelves for glassware. Even pots and pans—the largest and bulkiest of kitchen tools—require some depth in shelving, but not to the degree that standard shelving in cabinets provides. As proof, recall your childhood Saturday mornings. How many times did you awaken to the rattling of pots and pans as your mother searched for the skillet within a heap of assorted sizes and shapes of cookware?

There is a solution short of stripping out the existing cabinetry and starting—expensively—from scratch. You can reorganize, according to your own specifications and needs, the spacing arrangement of shelves, adding new shelves if necessary. Some items will require thirteen or more inches (33cm) of shelf space, while others need much less. The configuration you end up with will ideally be based on your own household goods and on your own needs.

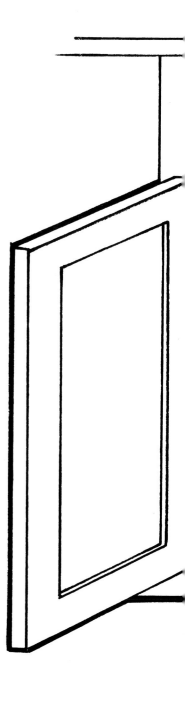

Look to the inside of cabinet doors as a possible area for storing pot lids, as shown here.

Spin-out, rotating racks fitted into the insides of cabinets make finding pots and pans as easy as spinning a lazy Susan.

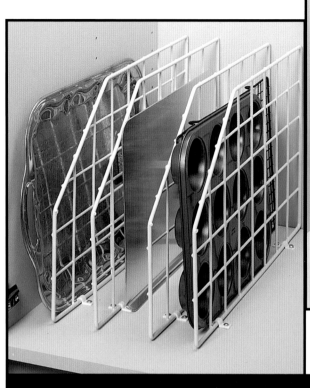

Storing Lids and Flat Cookware

Big, bulky pots and pans are easy to find when you need them, no matter how cramped to overflowing the kitchen cabinets are. It's the skinny, flat cookware items—slim skillets, cookie sheets, muffin pans, and, especially, pan lids—that get lost in the crammed quarters. Nothing can sour what started off as a cheerful bake day more quickly than having cookware come crashing out of the cabinets as a result of a frantic search for the single cookie sheet or the lid for the chocolate pot that's simmering on the stovetop.

Short of building a special lid or flat-cookware drawer or cabinet, you can customize the storage of these pieces with affordable container storage units. Long rectangular wire units house baking sheets and muffin tins; skinny skillets slide into a graduated tier of wire shelves; other plastic-coated wire units are designed to specifically accommodate lids.

Wire Shelving for Pantry Goods

Just as handily, wire shelving saves the storage day again when the pantry closet or cabinets simply aren't outfitted to store as many goods as you need them to. These portable, easy-to-assemble shelves can be configured in whatever design you need, depending on the size of the goods to be stored. Improve the way your existing pantry closet works, eliminating dead space, by dressing it out in wire shelving. Or, bring a wire shelf unit directly to the countertop or fill a vacant corner with a freestanding system.

Tip 4 Customize the interiors of your cupboards by outfitting shelves with plastic, rubber, or plastic-coated wire organizers geared specifically to your needs.

In addition to shelf dividers, an easy solution to getting more out of your existing shelf space is specialized plastic-coated wire shelf organizers. These devices can take virtually any flat shelf and give it a number of specialized functions, with adequate storage areas tailored to fit. Lazy Susans come in this form, allowing the convenience of a revolving presentation of your household goods on a shelf. Wire organizers for plates (almost like a dishwasher's scheme for organizing) turn a cupboard shelf into a sensible space with greatly reduced risks of breakage; with plates on end in such a storage unit, a very efficient use of shelf space can be made by situating tall glassware adjacent to the plate caddy. Don't hesitate to use wire organizer shelves anywhere in the kitchen. They come in all sizes and can fit in small spaces, and are extremely handy in grouping together such frequently used items as vitamins or cooking oils.

Other ready-made organizers that fit on the shelves right inside cabinets are made of plastic and rubber. Like the wire grids, these organizers compartmentalize the shelf contents, making it easier to lay one's hands on the potato chips without first having to pass by the soup cans.

Many times, room for additional shelf space is available in our kitchens, and we simply do not realize it. Take a good look at your kitchen to see if it's meeting its full potential for shelving.

A kitchen niche develops a finished architectural look when dressed with a freestanding cabinet that perfectly fits its dimensions. The furniture is ideal for housing unsightly household items in its drawers and for displaying flashier ones, such as this collection of colored pottery, on its exposed shelves.

Hidden Opportunities for Extra Shelving

A contemporary solution for an old-fashioned kitchen dictated tearing out dated cabinetry. In its place were put slender (and inexpensive) shelves for dinnerware and a hanging rack for cookware. A penchant for tidiness is necessary, however, for this storage option to be most effective.

Tip 5 Add shelves to the inside doors of pantries and cupboards when possible. When the main shelves are recessed sufficiently, this addition is extremely easy.

Wire shelf organizers can be found to completely outfit the pantry. A long, slender unit can affix to the back of the pantry door to accommodate small jars and bottles. Shelves of different sizes within the pantry organize soups, pastas, and other foods.

An important rule of thumb in planning pantry shelves is to keep them as shallow as possible—never more than two cans deep—otherwise, viewing food products becomes problematic, with jars and cans having to be lifted from the front to enable you to see what's hiding in the back. Instead, plan for U-shaped shelves (which turn the corner toward the

Every home has one: a kitchen drawer that opens only reluctantly, yawning and scraping along the way because of overflowing contents that are nothing short of unmitigated chaos. Drawers, however, are one of the easiest kitchen spaces to organize. And getting the drawer act together doesn't even take much time.

door hinge yet still utilize that dead space) that are only a single can deep; then, opposite the pantry's interior shelves, fit the back side of the door with additional shelves that slip into the recess formed by the U.

Tip 6 Create storage space with small, exposed shelves at the side ends of your cabinets or island counters.

When cabinets don't reach all the way to the ceiling, utilize the top space for storing handsome, large pieces that aren't used on a regular basis (big baskets, pottery, or other functional decorative pieces).

Tip 7 The space above the sink between cabinets is ideal for an efficient wireshelf organizer or a single wooden shelf.

49

Enhancing Architecture

Even though your home may not be outfitted with sleek built-in architectural storage features, don't ignore the possibilities of putting its existing architectural assets to work with a better choice of storage—friendly furnishings.

Architectural recesses, niches, and alcoves already draw the eye with their linear break from the room's norm. In these inherently interesting places, it only makes sense to store special pieces to which you want to draw focus.

A step-back wall is just wide enough for a stairstep furnishing that holds, pedestal-style, an individual objet d'art on each of its steps. Arranged on the diagonal, the pieces have more visual interest than collections lined up in uniform rows.

Easy-Does-It Architectural Ideas

Additional shelving is perhaps the easiest architectural change to make in the kitchen or dining room to gain storage. Finished shelves work best for the dining room, which, even in the most casual of decorating schemes, is usually more formal.

Tip 8 Explore a pair of vacant corners in your dining room for the possibility of building corner cupboards or, without the lower closed door cabinet, a corner shelving unit.

Corner cupboards or shelves in the dining room give a greater custom-look for the space and are an ideal place to showcase favorite decorative china or other tabletop pieces. While these architectural elements are common in traditional homes, they can also take on a sleek, contemporary look given the right application, such as faux granite decorative paint on the wood, or slick ebony laminate.

Tip 9 Add built-in plate racks or a wall of custom shelves above a dining room sideboard or console table to utilize precious wall space.

The space above furniture is often wasted space. Why not take that valuable space and, with a simple architectural addition of built-in plate racks or a custom shelving unit, treat yourself to much more room to display and store your dinner finery or favorite collections? This space will provide storage without impeding furniture arrangement—there's still plenty of room to put a waist-high furnishing against the wall.

Tip 10 Cut niches between the studs to provide cubbyholes for spices, pot holders, trivets, or other small items that need to be stored and organized in your kitchen.

An especially efficient area in which to carve architectural niches is above a built-in stove and to its sides. Large platters and other flat dinnerware used near the oven are handy stored atop the stove in a special niche. Side-pocket niches are convenient for items that are needed while cooking, such as salt and pepper or an assortment of different spices. These architectural additions are simple to create yourself—just cut out the drywall or plaster between the studs—to give a custom, tidy look to your kitchen.

Drawers

Tip 11 Organize drawers with trays, dividers, or other insets to compartmentalize contents in a logical, orderly fashion.

Start with common sense: put all like objects together; now, keep them that way with ready-made organizers. In addition to the basic flatware tray for forks, knives, and spoons, there are other plastic wire insets to fit additional needs. Try angled dividers supported by wooden wedges to create an easy-to-see spice rack within a standard kitchen drawer. The spice jars rest back on the wedges, with the bottoms of jars in one row leaning against the divider in the following row. If additional

Variation on a Theme: Built-in Bins

A form of cabinetry that works like a fruit cellar or food pantry is the transparent bin. Built out from the wall like a regular cabinet, the bin features a pull-up front (versus a door pulled open from one side), usually made of glass, for viewing the contents. Store perishables here, such as onions, carrots, and potatoes. In addition to serving an important functional role, such see-through produce bins add the natural color and charm of their contents to enhance the kitchen's appearance.

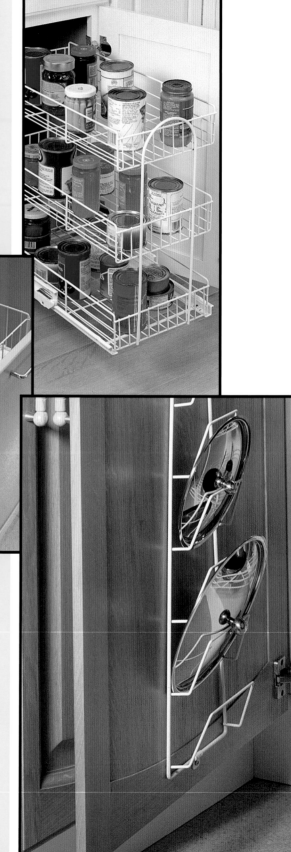

spice space isn't what you need, adapt the same principle for whatever it is you do need to store. Kitchen drawer organizers are available in such materials as handsome natural wicker and plastic-coated wire in a multitude of colors.

Tip 12 Turn a cabinet-size area into a huge sliding drawer instead of the conventional stationary cabinet.

Most people think that drawers for the kitchen deviate only a bit in size, with the smallest for flatware, the largest for bulkier kitchen utensils. But you can create more innovative and effective storage spaces by transforming cabinets, or the space typically designated for cabinets, into drawers. Large sliding drawers are ideal for housing an out-of-sight trash receptacle, a toaster, or any other often-used kitchen aid that's more easily accessed by sliding.

Often, storage can be improved without having to expand existing space. Instead, space can be put to better use through more efficient organization that increases storage capacity. Swivel-out wire ledges (left) can fit inside cabinets, making better use of vertical space, while pullout wire drawers (above) can transform an inefficient, skinny pantry into one that's hardworking.

Cabinets

One all-important question must be answered before thinking about cabinets for the kitchen: do you want their contents to be hidden or exposed? There is a movement toward a visual/aesthetic appreciation of culinary products—apart from their utilitarian value—almost as though they were accessories or collectibles. This trend has given rise to a burgeoning number of glass-front or open cabinets in today's homes.

Tip 13 How organized you want your kitchen to appear should be a consideration in deciding between glass or wooden-door cabinets. Be honest with yourself: if you are not inherently neat, it is best to hide your cabinet contents behind wooden doors.

There's no disputing that colorful contents in open cabinets serve to warm the kitchen. But sometimes, the look is too frantic; instead of the well-organized effect you'd hoped for, you have an impression of a cache of thrown-together goods. When you choose open cabinets, you will need to practice temperance in how you use them. It won't do to cram foodstuffs together or stack items for quickie convenience with no thought to how they will look, because they are always on display. You have to work harder to stay orderly. In addition, the grime that is sometimes found on top of even the most hygienic of chefs condiment bottles and jars must be continually cleaned if exposed cabinets are the choice. Vigilance in cleanliness is required.

In an extremely small kitchen, or especially in an antique kitchen in which the addition of cabinetry would spoil the original look, there's often a dearth of space to stash bulky yet essential pots and pans. The idea of overhead hanging racks was conceived for kitchens such as these. Not only do the hanging racks free up the existing cabinets for other storage purposes, but they also add an element of charm to the room, drawing the eye upward to what otherwise might be a visually bland space.

Suspended Storage

Tip 14 The most efficient kitchens utilize air space for storage, with racks for pots and pans suspended from the ceiling, hanging tiered baskets for vegetables, racks for hanging barware upside down, and wall-mounted wire units for hanging coffee cups or utensils.

In a category of their own as a kitchen storage unit are racks, hooks, baskets, pegs, and sleeves that can be hung from the ceiling or mounted onto the wall to hold clutter in suspension. One of the best and most commonly used storage inventions for the kitchen is the overhead pots-and-pans rack. Not only is this device easy to install (two screws in the ceiling will get the job done), but it organizes your cookware without taking up precious cabinet space. It leaves room to store ice cream machines, bread machines, or any other large gadget in the leftover cabinet space. Just be sure you dangle your best cookware from the rack—top-dollar brands or anything copper looks especially good. Rectangular or circular racks are both widely available.

Another excellent overhead idea is to utilize a ready-made organizer (or a homemade one) to hang wine and bar glasses upside down above standing height in your kitchen. Storing barware in this manner leaves more room for other glassware to spread out—without being stacked or jammed together—in the cabinets. This storage solution also adds warmth to the appearance of your kitchen.

Overhead pot-and-pan racks aren't as standardized as you might think: custom creations utilize highly textured materials—braided iron, for example—and assorted shapes from rectangular to round to make artistic statements of their own.

Long hooks straddled over a single wall-mounted shelf create an accessible storage space for pots and pans, putting them above precious cabinet space and getting them off counter surfaces.

Unless you live in a new house with a forward-thinking kitchen design, you probably don't have the luxury of built-ins to accommodate your sorted recyclables. But the good news is that an environmentally correct lifestyle doesn't have to be chaotic or messy. The manufacturers of portable organizers have answered consumer demand with an array of options to fit your kitchen.

58

Next to overhead pot racks, one of the kitchen's most popular suspension storage units is the hanging wire mesh basket. Dangling from a chain, this item features a tier of baskets—usually three—that are handy for soon-to-be-used produce. This organizer is not the best solution for long-term storage of produce, however, as exposure to air and light will accelerate ripening.

Small plastic-coated wire organizers that can be mounted to the wall also provide a space to hang cooking spoons. Outfitted with hooks, these organizers can even be used to present coffee cups suspended by their handles. Don't forget wall-mounted paper-towel dispensers and other like products, which put in-demand kitchen items within convenient reach, yet off countertops and out of the way.

Cases of soft drinks, mass quantities of on-sale items, huge bags of pet foods, and other storable kitchenwares find happy homes in the wire baskets of carts, which can either be left stationary or outfitted with casters and rolled out of the way when not needed. Add a laminate top to the upper basket and you've created yet another flat surface for working or for storing assorted kitchen gear.

Additional ideas for using ready-made storage units in the kitchen include storing cookbooks and recipe files in a wire office unit—a five-runner cart with files at the top, and shallow and deeper drawers for various sizes of cookbooks and cooking magazines. Originally intended for home-office use, the unit is a natural for the storage needs of the cookbook-accruing chef.

Also explore the possibilities of creating additional food storage space from stackable drawers, which can be placed on top of the refrigerator, on a portable microwave, or on the counter-

Countertops

Sometimes it's easy to forget the obvious. In a discussion of kitchen storage, that might mean ignoring countertops as storage space. Counters provide far more than a place to perform food preparation tasks. There is room left over for "stuff." Use it wisely.

By using uniform containers—clear plastic jars, stacked plastic boxes, glass bottles, or stoneware pottery—the entire kitchen countertop area can be outlined with storage goods without looking messy or cluttered.

top. Drawers come in different sizes, including a jumbo size that works well for large quantities of foodstuffs.

Tip 15 Make it easier to sort and store recyclables by tossing them into the roomy wire baskets of a kitchen cart.

Consider wire-basket carts for sorting recyclables, too. The deep baskets can accommodate newspapers, plastics, glass, and aluminum with room to spare. The lightweight baskets can be removed from the cart and taken straight to the recycling center, where the contents can be dumped, without the trouble of having to switch containers. While a standard, multipurpose wire-basket cart can be enlisted for this service, some companies offer specialty recycling units that feature three extra-deep baskets for newspapers, bottles, and aluminum or plastics.

Tip 16 Create a pantry by stacking wire drawers in a rolling cart and filling them with groceries.

For a kitchen that's missing a closet pantry altogether or one that is sadly lacking in adequate pantry space, various configurations of portable, ready-made wire stacking drawers, baskets, and bins allow you to create your own pantry storage area for canned and packaged foods without the trouble and expense of reconstructing your kitchen. Because these units can be pulled out from a cart, the pantry rule of "one can deep" does not apply; the full depth of a stacking drawer can be filled with soup cans, and retrieval can still be easy, with viewing possible from above. When it's time to unload groceries, simply wheel the cart up to the bags.

FOUR

Living Spaces

In the living room, storage can take an elegant form that's not easily recognizable as functional. A striking case in point is this bamboo ladder—a collectible in its own right. When its rungs are crossed with boards, the focal point of the room becomes a functional furnishing for storing an array of books and collectibles. It even serves the function of a side table when mounted with a clip-on reading lamp.

As the centers of leisure time, both formal and informal, the living and family rooms require thoughtfully conceived storage solutions. These are the rooms where the family flops down, dropping pretense and, to a degree, decorum, after a long day at work or school; and these are the rooms where guests are entertained—where vital impressions are made that can influence the career and social life of the hosts.

Because the living and family rooms are where most of a family's free time is spent while at home, and where they do most entertaining, these spaces should look good. But while visually expressing the home-owner's personality and preferred style, these rooms must also meet the real needs of the household. This means that storage provisions—the working core or machinery of a home—are an unavoidable requirement for these spaces. The challenge in these public rooms is to find storage solutions that are both highly functional and subtle, disrupting the integrity of the interior design as little as possible. At their best, the storage innovations will actually add to the decor, serving to unify, balance, and enhance the spaces.

While floor plans of many homes include both casual family rooms and more formal living rooms, that isn't always the case. In many homes today, there is a single room serving both functions—as a hangout for "just family" as well as a retreat for entertaining friends or business associates. Storage in such a room must be thoroughly thought out because the dual formal/informal functions require a great deal of stashing and organizing of household items that are essential to getting not one but two jobs done. The double storage challenge becomes even tougher when a compromise on aesthetics—even taking just a little license on the laws of design and what looks good—is unwanted.

The goal of this chapter is to identify and inspire storage alternatives that are both attractive and efficient, and that will hold up even under the demanding circumstances of a combination living/ family room. Because of the overlapping functions of family and living rooms, the storage needs of both spaces are addressed together. For even when the two rooms fill somewhat different roles, many of the furnishings and other lifestyle accoutrements are the same.

Magazines and books, for example, are common to both rooms. Often, home electronic equipment—TVs, stereos, and even entire home theaters—is found in both family and living rooms. The CDs, tapes, and videos, as well as the electronic equipment, all need an orderly and accessible, yet attractive place in the room. Wet bars (and all the stemware, bottles, and accessories that go with them) can also be found in either a family room or a living room. A wide variety of collectibles, as well as more pedestrian items such as tax records, mail, and toys, are often inhabitants of these living spaces as well. And the list of essentials that require storage spaces of their own goes on.

Architectural built-ins, furniture especially designed for storage, and portable organizers can ensure that every item in a home's living space fits neatly into the room's scheme, with an easy-to-locate place of its own. Available in infinite styles and finishes, these storage options can be carefully selected to work with any room's decorating scheme, forming a seamless part of the home's decor.

Architectural Answers

Unless you are among the rare breed that actually thrives on the chaos and disorder of a house under reconstruction, knocking out walls and reshaping the lines of your family or living room probably doesn't hold much appeal as a viable approach to getting organized. Finances will figure into your decisions, too, acting as a deterrent when a significant structural makeover is being considered.

Short of ripping out the rafters, however, there are architectural redos for the public spaces of the home that require minimal physical change yet yield many aesthetic and utilitarian rewards. All it takes to get started is a good eye.

Although it's true that a good eye for design is something bestowed at birth, it can also be cultivated. Like any other skill, this one requires practice and homework.

Paneled doors add rich architectural elegance on the underside of a staircase—but they also make a clever cache for a world of storage items.

Tip 1 When considering architectural built-ins, hone an eye for design by starting a clip file of outstanding examples culled from home design and architectural magazines.

You can begin by flipping through the pages of home design magazines and books, taking special note of built-in features. Which family/living room accommodates books and other items that you need to store in a manner that's most pleasing to you? Are there any homes that incorporate particularly interesting storage solutions that you think will be able to work in your home? Start a notebook of clippings that illustrate your favorite spaces. As you pursue this research, you will begin to observe certain commonalities among your favorite rooms, such as overhead shelving scaled to permit furniture placement against the walls, closets tucked neatly in a corner, built-in seating/storage units, or the symmetrical balance of built-in bookshelves situated on the flanks of a center fireplace.

Once you've established what you like and have seen that it works, you're ready to apply your lessons to your own home. Here, a good eye translates as simple common sense. If your fireplace is off-center to the side of a wall, for example, the symmetrical bookshelves you admired in magazines won't deliver the same promise. Attempting to construct fireside shelving that's not evenly balanced may look fine, and may even appear artistically asymmetrical—but it also may result in an awkwardness that suggests something's naggingly askew.

Opposite: This sitting room retains its simplicity thanks to effective storage: built-in closets keep things simple by hiding items behind closed doors.

A room with a center-walled fireplace presents an architectural storage opportunity that's easy to construct. Sustaining perfect symmetry for the room are bookshelves and cabinets built on either side of the fireplace.

Tip 2 Always sketch your favorite ideas for built-in storage into a drawing of your room before going to the trouble of construction and, potentially, suffering the regrets it can sometimes bring.

When your existing architecture doesn't closely match that of your example, don't automatically dismiss the built-in storage idea as impossible. Instead, give it the benefit of the doubt by first sketching it onto paper in a drawing of your room. If it looks odd on paper, don't continue. But if

you like what you see in the thumbnail rendering, it's likely you will the finished results in your love home.

Pay close attention to how built-ins are scaled and positioned in the rooms in your clip file. Just because a laminate finish catches your eye doesn't mean you can slap a built-in entertainment unit with laminate shelving into place just anywhere. Think about some of the homes you've entered in which built-in features didn't work, such as a room where the bookcases perched peculiarly beside a door, sticking out like the proverbial sore thumb. When considering any alteration in your home's architecture, no matter how minor, keep in mind the overall picture. Be sure your addition will harmoniously blend into the natural lines of the room. It should compliment, not detract from, the existing architecture.

Scale is just as important as positioning. The window seat with underneath storage that looks so charming in a magazine's featured home may make your small living room look cramped. Consider the dimensions of your room and those of the built-in. An enclosed structure such as a window seat visually reduces the size of the room more than open shelving with "air." Consider only additions that will preserve a sense of perceived, if not actual, spaciousness and will not notably diminish the room's size.

Tip 3 Evaluate open or closed storage according to the uniformity and overall attractiveness of the items to be stored.

There is one general question that should be addressed before deciding to add an architectural built-in to a family room or living room (this same question should be repeated while solving storage problems in every room of the home): should the storage be open or closed?

If access is essential, such as for a CD or video library that you want to scan quickly, open storage is your best option. Also, consider open storage when the objects are like members of a set. A handful of quilts, for instance, neatly stacked on open shelves can constitute its own attractive display; a single quilt plus a mishmash of odds and ends would usually be better stored behind closed doors.

Speaking of . . .

Most home owners have accepted the idea that some of the home's functions—such as providing a space for listening to recorded music—are pursuits whose accoutrements are valid for display. In other words, most of us have made peace with the presence of stereo speakers alongside our more visual home furnishings.

But not everyone chooses to grant equal eye time to mechanical devices. In those instances, a little cover-up goes a long way. The mesh panels of stereo speakers are easy targets for a fool-the-eye camouflage. Paint the speaker covers to create whatever trompe l'oeil effect you want. If the stereo speakers are sharing space on the book shelf, a natural solution is a little concealing "book" paint, as shown here.

Tip 4 If your family or living room is wide enough, line one wall entirely with closets that are attractively hidden behind sliding louvered doors.

Although adding a single-door closet for storage isn't often an option in a family room or living room because it cuts up space, an entire wall of closet storage is a different matter. Sliding louvered doors, with their horizontal wood patterns, and stained or painted to match the remaining walls, actually create additional visual interest in a room. Outfitted with organizers to meet your needs exactly or custom-designed with shelves, drawers, and hanging spaces, such a closet wall can hold virtually everything imaginable, from winter wraps to wrapping paper. Toys, board games, financial papers, extra blankets, and pillows for snuggling up on the sofa on a chilly evening—all can find a place in the closet wall. And this architectural solution requires little work besides shopping for the perfect doors.

Tip 5 Construct permanent shelves and cabinets on either side of a centrally placed fireplace.

Some living rooms equipped with beautiful fireplaces placed squarely in the center of a wall don't take full architectural advantage of the opportunity this provides. Building in bookshelves on either side of the fireplace not only provides precious storage space, but gives a finished, crafted look to the room.

Opposite: These sliding doors work to hide a wet bar from view when not in use. Building a closet in dead space is a great way to make that space come alive, all for the price of appropriate doors.

When designing your own entertainment center, keep in mind a balance of exposed and closed spaces. Leave enough open shelf compartments for displaying books and collectibles; hide the mechanics of entertainment behind cabinet doors.

Since you're building the shelves yourself, customize the spaces between them to fit your needs. On the lower section, think about building cabinets to hide less visually pleasing items behind closed doors.

Tip 6 Use decorative molding to finish off a home entertainment center you have built yourself. Incorporate a laminated finish and decorative molding to give the wall unit a built-in, custom look.

Tip 7 Consider a room divider outfitted with cabinets for storage.

Another relatively simple architectural improvement that adds storage space to the public rooms of the home is a room divider, which can serve as a great place for tossing all sorts of essential clutter. These units work well when the living room or family room feeds onto a hallway, as they help to define the main living space. Take care not to make the height of a room divider too tall, however, which would cut the room's amount of perceived space. You may want to paint or stain the cabinets to match the walls so that the unit blends harmoniously into the room. Or, consider creating a sharp focal point by using a bright, unexpected color (but be certain that it is one that works with your room's palette).

Tip 8 If hiding electronics is your aim, consider building simple shelves for the equipment, then hanging a sliding custom mural on a rod.

Finding a Place for Fun

Along with the enhanced home-entertainment opportunities that new electronic technology has brought, there comes a problem: where to put the large-screen TV, VCR, CD player, computer, and Nintendo, and all the videos, CDs, and disks that go along with them. For the living room or family room that is well stocked in electronic diversions, building a custom center of shelves and cabinets is the ideal solution. (CD racks and stacking stereo components may look fine in a room, but too many of these freestanding pieces can create a choppy effect that destroys the room's unity.)

Select a wall that lends itself well to furniture placement and has a conversation area nearby that can be arranged around the entertainment center. Space eye-level shelves to fit your viewing screens, then create smaller vertical shelves above and below to accommodate their accessories. If computer games are a favorite pastime, relegate the terminal to an office, but include it in the central living space as part of the entertainment center. If space permits, leave room for a few book-size shelves for storing either books or collectibles.

As with bookshelves, an entertainment center can also include cabinets at floor level for stashing a potpourri of items. Drawers can be added, too, without detracting from the frontal appearance of the unit.

In conceptualizing your entertainment unit, take some creative license. Just because store-bought furnishings span a uniform height doesn't mean the various components of one that you build yourself must. Create a center section that's half the height of the two flanking sides, then cap it with a favorite wall sculpture or painting. Or, create a stair-step effect, building component shelving higher and higher from the center.

One of the more unusual and appealing solutions to home media storage requires not only shelf construction but art. A wrought-iron rod suspended above built-in shelves can serve as host to a sliding mural or painted canvas. When the TV is not in use, all that greets the eye is art. Simply slide the canvas (or board) to one side when it's entertainment time. Unless there's an artist (or even a stenciler) in the family, the only restraint to this architectural

Television sets and miscellaneous items you'd rather not have on view all day long take cover at the flick of your wrist with pull-down matchstick blinds.

innovation is expense. In addition to commissioning an artwork, metalworkers must be hired to make a rod to size.

Tip 9 Build a banquette sofa with below-the-seat storage drawers.

Especially in contemporary rooms, banquette seating is an immediate statement of style. Its streamlined form articulates the contemporary ideal, but with the right upholstery fabrics, throw pillows, and wood finish, this architectural addition can also venture into more traditional or country styles. For the home owner who needs storage space, this solution is worth the money, making the bulkiest furnishing in the room—the sofa—work overtime as a cache for small storables.

Tip 10 Build a window seat that extends across an entire wall in which there is a window, with lift-up or sliding doors providing storage below.

One of the most attractive features of any room is its windows. Adding a window seat below the living room or family room window is a sure way of enhancing that area as a focal point. Any style can be conveyed here through appropriately chosen fabric coverings for cushions. When covered with cushy throw pillows, the area becomes a charming area to bask in streams of sunlight with a good book.

To construct an easy-to-make window seat yourself, consider centering a lift-up door below the seating platform, then flanking it with sliding cabinet doors. In one fell swoop, an entire wall becomes a vehicle for both storage and seating.

Armed with Armoires

Armoires aren't just for the bedroom. These valuable storage cupboards have long been recognized as worthy of the living room. And these furnishings aren't merely functional: they're often among the best-looking pieces in the home. Because of an armoire's large scale, it can also provide architecture where there is none, creating a major focal point in a room that has no fireplace, interesting moldings, or built-in bookshelves.

As a storage area for home electronics, armoires have an additional advantage: when the doors are closed, the equipment is out of view, and all that can be seen is a fine piece of furniture.

Before purchasing an armoire or any tall, freestanding cupboard, know the dimensions of the equipment that you want to store inside it. Be sure that your selection has adequate depth to accommodate your electronics.

Since only new armoires come already outfitted or custom-fitted to your specifications, consider hiring a professional cabinetmaker to finish the inside space of an old or antique armoire to your liking. And certainly don't begin drilling holes in the back of an antique furnishing and risk ruining the piece's integrity, unless you are well versed in the properties of wood and have sufficient carpentry skills.

Chances are good there is space inside an armoire to store your TV, VCR, and stereo components, as well as the videos, tapes, and CDs that you'll be using. The advantages of containing all paraphernalia in one location are appealing, freeing up the remainder of the room for other functions.

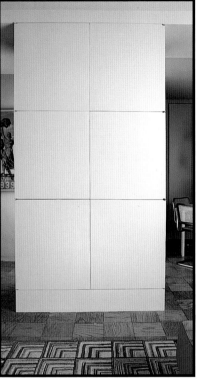

Armoires employed in the living room can take any style, from country primitive (left) to sleek contemporary (above), to work with the room's overall style.

One of the most space-saving forms of storage goes straight to the wall, with built-in shelves and cabinets. To house a variety of different items and create the most powerful visual impact, vary the cabinetry, keeping some shelves behind closed doors, others exposed, and still others behind glass panes.

Furnishings

One of the simplest answers to solving storage problems in the public spaces of the home is to buy the right furniture. Why waste square footage with space-guzzling furnishings, no matter how aesthetically pleasing, if they don't address your priority for storage capacity? Case goods come in all styles and prices. In other words, when it comes to furnishings, there's something for everyone.

Tip 11 Choose cabinet-fronted sofa tables and shadow-box cocktail tables to provide both hidden and visible storage.

Instead of backing your sofa with an open-legged sofa table, supply the same amount of tabletop display space and take up exactly the same amount of floor space with a sofa table made with cabinets. With cocktail tables, the same principle is at work. A number of different top-selling cocktail table designs are glass-topped shadow boxes that can display collections of boxes, pipes, fragile old books, fishing lures—anything in need of storage that you don't mind being showcased.

In a traditional living room, a small antique wooden chest with drawers provides small-item storage while doubling as a side table for an elegant tufted chair and ottoman.

A collection of trunks serves as arresting art in its own right, especially when arranged in a staggered-height, stair-step display. But even better, the interior of each trunk is imminently functional, perfect for storing household items.

Tip 12 Utilize antique trunks as coffee tables and old wooden crates as accent tables.

While a number of case goods can be found for storage needs among manufacturers' standard furnishing lines, other options exist that are a little less standard. Even in a contemporary family room, an antique trunk or painted chest used as a coffee table can add a whimsical touch of warmth, while hiding a multitude of memorabilia.

The old wooden shipping crates that bear product names can also provide a punchy accent to a living space. At the same time, these crates are an excellent place to store kids' school papers or other keepsakes. Instead of merely taking up space, they can be topped with candlesticks, a plant, or any accessory that needs a home, to create an appealing still life.

75

Even a light and breezy wicker-furnished living room can include furniture that serves the dual purpose of table and trunk, as does the wicker side table shown here.

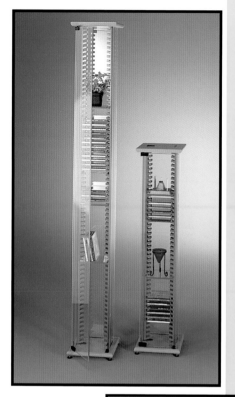

CD Solutions

There are many special units available that are designed just for housing CDs and videos: video/CD columns, stackable media shelves, wire CD towers, CD bookends, stackable plastic video/CD tubs, and others.

Portable, affordable units designed just for housing CDs and videos are one of the greatest recent inventions. A quick fix, they can be found in almost any shape and can be configured into vertical or horizontal stacks of almost any dimension. First, determine which units will fit your space, then choose one that will look best and blend most harmoniously with your room decor.

Columns, painted in a wide range of colors, are the most finished, permanent choice—and are also the most expensive. Because of their narrow shape, it's an easy matter to add on a second, third, or fourth column as your video/CD library grows. The least permanent solution is see-through plastic media tubs, which can be added to and stacked one on top of the other as storage needs increase. While the tubs offer flexibility and the most affordability, they will not be mistaken for furniture. Still, they keep the room looking neat and offer a practical system of organization.

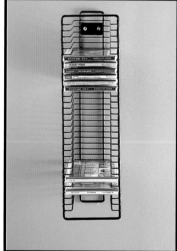

Portable Organizers

When the budget is tight but storage needs are great, portable organizers are the best solution. For a fraction of the cost of adding architectural built-ins or purchasing fine furniture, portable organizers can be used in the living or family room to serve as caddies for all your needs. Because these units are designed especially for storage, many for specific types of storage, they often afford a more organized system than standard furniture or even built-ins.

Tip 13 Look for assemble-it-yourself modular bookcases and wall systems when ready-made furniture is cost-prohibitive.

The same manufacturers that bring you stackable boxes and portable organizing units also offer a middle-of-the-road alternative—furniture units that you assemble yourself—ideal for the needs of the family room and living room. Most are very affordable.

Available in a modern palette of color choices, these units are not constructed of fine, grained wood, but laminated particleboard. But when an attractive look that accomplishes the task at hand is more important than pedigree, they are an alluring solution.

Like other organizers, these units are open-ended: as your storage needs increase, additional units can be added to the modular system. For many, these systems have more appeal than architectural built-ins or fine furnishings because they allow for room to grow.

Handpainted nested wooden boxes create a beautiful sofa-side shape when stacked one atop the other, allowing the boxes' contents to remain full of mystery.

 Tip 14 **Don't forget the small organizers—bins, boxes, tubs, and baskets—that can organize small items that are frequently used in the main living spaces of the home.**

There occasionally comes a time, while lounging around the family room, when you want to take a walk into yesteryear by looking at old photographs. But you don't want photographs cluttering your coffee table and sofa all the time. Portable organizers—albums, boxes, file systems—arrange your keepsakes in an orderly fashion and can be left out on a table or put inside the top of a closet when you're done. These portable organizers come in a wide range of sizes to accommodate the items you need to store.

Baskets make great caddies for magazines. Boxes (decorative ones, not cardboard) are good stashes for matches, decks of cards, or anything you might need in your main living space but don't want out in full view all the time.

77

FIVE

Bathrooms

Like the kitchen, every bathroom has special storage demands. Inadequate attention to those demands results in a room that's a constant irritant. But it doesn't have to be that way. Even small bathrooms can be outfitted with storage units tailored to the room's size and shape and to the home owner's needs. Cleaning out old toiletries and organizing items in related groups goes a long way to solving what seems to be a storage crisis.

Despite the trend toward big, luxurious bathrooms, most homes remain ill equipped when it comes to storage space in the bath. Even when a home's bathrooms outnumber its bedrooms (which is becoming more and more common among upper-echelon home owners), there's often still a degree of awkwardness concerning storage.

The problem stems from the necessity of storing so many items with so many different functions—toiletries, cleaning supplies, medicines, tissues, makeup, blow-dryers, and towels. But despite the large number of things requiring storage, many home owners desire a streamlined bathroom that appears clutter-free, more so than any other room in the house. It is little wonder that these two goals appear, much to the home owner's frustration, mutually exclusive.

When remodeling is an option, storage becomes far less problematic, for knocking down walls to expand the bath space allows for storage to be tailored to your precise needs. For most of us, though, that isn't an alternative. Either there's no room for the expansion because existing hallways and adjacent rooms are not expendable, or the costs are prohibitive. Instead, we must make the most of what we have.

Instead of being daunted by the task, look to the positive: with the possible exception of the kitchen, more specialized storage aids exist for the bath than for any other room. With a wide range to choose from, there are solutions that will work for you.

Cleansing the Bath

The first step in improving storage in the bath is to begin a housecleaning campaign, eliminating all unnecessary or infrequently used items from your inventory of bathroom products.

If you're like most people, your bathroom contains a cornucopia of unessentials. For some reason, you haven't taken the time to toss out those items you don't need. A glance in the medicine chest might reveal a number of outdated prescription medications that you not only can but should throw away. Old bottles of nail polish, with encrusted caps that are hard to open, have also earned their place in the garbage heap. Old makeup, cleansing products, aftershaves, and colognes that for some reason weren't up to your standards should be summarily dismissed. White towels gone gray as well as tattered washcloths can be recycled as cleaning supplies—and scratched from your list of bathroom items in need of storage. Once you've lightened the load, seeking storage solutions will become infinitely more manageable.

Tip 1 Review the spacing between shelves in existing cabinets, then alter heights to fit your needs.

Like the kitchen, the bathroom is usually outfitted with cabinetry for storage that doesn't meet its full potential because of poorly positioned shelves. If you regularly purchase family-size packages of hygiene products, you need a tall space in which to store them. One possibility would be to remove a shelf from a bathroom cupboard to avoid having to cram in products on their sides.

Instead of stacking all the bath towels in a single vertical tower that falls each time you pull out a towel from anywhere but the top, divide and conquer. Add a shelf to the cabinet to allow two manageable stacks. Create a shelf just for hand towels and washcloths.

Tip 2 Recruit large, attractive baskets to store frequently used materials that you don't mind having on view.

It can be embarrassing to have the roll of toilet tissue emptied by a houseguest, who must either search your bathroom for another roll, ask you to locate one, or do without. For guests' comfort, and for your own, why not ensure that a plentiful supply is always on hand? A large woven basket, which can be placed on the floor in plain sight, becomes an attractive room accessory when employed for this storage purpose.

Baskets can also be enlisted as a convenience for storing hand towels and washcloths—again, so you don't have to go looking and guests don't have to ask. Hairbrushes, combs, and

Straightening Up Your Act

Already existing in your bathroom is some kind of storage capacity—perhaps not as much as you'd like, but enough to work with. With your bathroom paraphernalia pared down, improving storage may be as simple as organizing the spaces already in existence. The following ideas will help.

☐ Compartmentalized wire trays can be inserted into vanity drawers, creating a tidy system that separates cotton balls from razors, cotton swabs from facial creams.

☐ Cleaning products that compete for cabinet space with lotions and other personal pampering products can be relegated to a wire shelf hanging on the inside panel of a cabinet door.

☐ For the cabinet below the sink, plastic stackable tubs make use of the cabinet's height while providing a handy retrieval mechanism.

☐ Instead of searching for enclosed storage space, make use of the exposed surfaces in your bath—the tops of vanities, the toilet tank's top, and any open shelving. A bath can acquire character through orderly displays of products. Handsomely packaged cosmetics and colorful towels, in particular, can inject a personal punch.

☐ Sometimes existing vanities and cabinets provide enough storage, but a moisture problem prevents you from storing some items, such as towels, where you would like. Rather than going to the trouble of adding storage space for nonwaterproof items, consider making your current storage dry with tighter-fitting doors or waterproof liners that can be tacked or laid onto overhead shelves.

An Organizer for Every Object

Organizers made of plastic-coated wire and solid plastic are available in an array of colors to serve specialized functions in the bath. Shampoo and soap caddies can be hung from the showerhead, eliminating the clutter of bottles, tubes, and bars from the shower floor or side of the bath. Other versions can be attached onto the tub itself. Wall-mounted toothbrush holders a good solution that doesn't need improving.

Wire-coated plastic shelves, which come in a rainbow of hues and are great for generic storage use in any room of the house, are ideal in the bathroom. Hung in the dead space above the tub, these inexpensive racks provide as much storage room as a wall of cabinets. And they cost a fraction as much, without devouring a single inch of actual floor space.

Towel racks and wall hooks are other commonly used organizers, and could be put to even greater use. The back of the bathroom door, for instance, can become host to bathrobes and towels by the simple application of hooks (many of which feature motifs to fit with the room's decor, such as stars or ivy). Search out the dead space in your bath, whether it's the back of the door or the corner by the toilet, then put it to work with wall-mounted organizers that accommodate your items.

Clear plastic or glass canisters and jars provide space for toiletries. Everyone recalls the bath beads stored in this manner in grandmother's house, but just because an idea isn't new doesn't mean it is antiquated. And there is a design statement in number: multiple glass canisters become a focal point that's more potent than any single container by itself.

clips are logical partners in a basket of their own, placed attractively on a vanity top or even on top of a toilet tank.

Tip 3 Add a flounced fabric skirt to a pedestal sink to create hidden space for cleaning products or grooming accessories.

A freestanding pedestal sink leaves little hope for storage, short of removing the fixture and replacing it with a cabinet-front vanity—or does it? The area beneath the sink can go to work as storage space for you with the simple addition of a gathered fabric skirt that extends to the floor.

Reflecting your bathroom's palette while adding interesting pattern, a skirt brings a soft, romantic charm to the room, which the fixture alone could never hope to attain. If enough matching or coordinated fabric is purchased, the windows and perhaps even the tub (as a shower curtain) can be dressed to create a pulled-together look for the entire room. If your home features a cottage-style or romantic theme, this solution is especially worth considering.

Tip 4 Build an open-faced medicine cabinet or niche between the studs of the bathroom wall to store grooming accessories.

The simplest way of adding a small amount of built-in storage to the bath is to cut into the wall, between the studs, to create a recessed storage niche. If a medicine cabinet isn't already built into the room, this is an easy way to create one. Decorative molding around the edges produces a finished, always-been-there look.

Skirting a pedestal vanity sink creates a hidden area for stashing bathroom cleaning products or necessary toiletries.

Tip 5 Add a prebuilt vanity to customize a standard bath fixture.

Ready-made vanities (cabinets encasing standard bathroom sinks) come in a full range of styles, materials, shapes, and prices, making it possible to avoid the expense of custom cabinetry. Be aware that here, as with any other purchase, you get what you pay for. If you plan on staying in your house for a while, think about opting for a higher-end product that you can be proud of. Some of the options are tile, plastic laminate, marble, and wood. Be aware that most of these prebuilt structures are made from particleboard, covered with veneer.

When shopping for your vanity, come armed with your bathroom dimensions. Many retailers and lumberyards now offer a computerized

Surround Yourself with Storage

If the space between your bathtub and the other fixtures is adequate, with plenty of walking room to spare, you may want to build a wooden surround along the side of your tub, enclosing it almost like a hot tub's decking. The linear addition shouldn't be much more than a foot (30.4 cm) deep, or too much of the room's depth will be reduced. But what the surround lacks in depth, it more than compensates for in length. Spanning the entire length of the tub, it can open at the front on a hinge, providing space for small bath accessories inside.

service that allows you to input your dimensions along with a vanity option, then view a three-dimensional picture of your bathroom as it would appear with the new vanity installed. After seeing the computer image, you may decide that the vanity that initially caught your eye isn't all you imagined it to be. You can actually design your bathroom on the spot, thanks to this new technology.

Review photographs of bathrooms in design magazines before developing a precise picture of what you want. Instead of the expected square or rectangular vanity, your bath may benefit from a more unusually shaped unit such as a triangle or a curve. Besides adding visual interest, these odd shapes sometimes make better use of space, thus providing more efficient storage.

To keep a sleekly designed bathroom streamlined and uncluttered, a few well-chosen baskets functioning as accessories can serve as receptacles for bath towels and magazines.

Customizing the tub: space permitting, consider adding a shelf or extending the tub at both ends with a frame in order to create practical storage areas for towels and toiletries. This solution is optimal when the bathroom's vertical wall space for cabinets or closets is lacking or minimal—due, perhaps, to a long-slung window.

85

Tip 6 Hang a premade cabinet above the toilet that reaches all the way to the ceiling.

Often, finding dead space in a bathroom is as simple as snooping around the fixtures. Just because these essentials are fixed components in the room doesn't mean that the space surrounding them is sacrosanct.

Put this space to use—especially the space above the toilet. Instead of hanging a small rack for hand towels here, utilize it more thoroughly: hang a premade cabinet that reaches all the way to the ceiling. Just be sure to leave enough room above the toilet to allow space for removal of the tank top. An open-front cabinet in this often-ignored space is a great place for storing items such as bath linens, tissues, and even magazines.

Tip 7 Build an easy do-it-yourself shelving unit above the toilet to add architecture as well as storage to the room.

Though it may look complicated, a custom-built shelving cabinet that surrounds the toilet actually requires few steps to make. Using two-by-fours, surround the toilet from the floor to ceiling with a permanently affixed frame. Then, mount tempered-glass shelves on shelf standards with clips. The shelf heights can be adjusted according to your changing needs.

Tip 8 Turn the corners: create storage in these dead spaces with diagonal shelves, which can add needed storage in even the smallest of bathrooms.

You don't have to be a skilled cabinetmaker or even a weekend carpenter to add a little architecture and storage space to your bathroom. It's likely that at least one corner of your bathroom is unoccupied, ready to be put to some worthy creative use.

Triangular-cut boards of wood that fit into the right angles of the corner are all you need, along with a hammer and nails. Make an architectural tower of corner shelves, spanning from floor to ceiling, if you choose; or create upper shelves only, if that's more to your liking.

Tip 9 When floor space isn't tight but storage is, augment your storage with a closet of open shelves, compartments, and hanging space hidden neatly behind louvered or solid sliding or bifold doors.

Cheaper than expensive cabinetry, a closet provides even more storage while still presenting the sleek look of an enclosed space. The only real drawback is the amount of space it cuts from the room: when a bathroom is already narrow, adding a closet that juts into the limited walking space creates more of a nuisance than it's worth. On the positive side, such a closet requires little in the way of construction and offers hanging space and more vertical stacking space than cabinets can provide.

A double-door hall closet can be a flexible space to accommodate everything from sheets to shoe polish. Keep contents of each shelf consistent for sensible storage.

Outfitted with casters for easy movement, stack-based utility carts are ideal companions for the laundry room as well as the bathroom.

Tip 10 Consider replacing the front doors of existing pieces of cabinetry instead of replacing the entire cabinets when undertaking a bathroom expansion that includes adding new pieces. Dressed in their new cabinet fronts, your old cabinets will perfectly match the newly added cabinetry of your choice.

When a fresh look is all that's needed for the bathroom, new cabinet fronts are an ideal option. But their function goes far beyond the merely decorative. When a bathroom is being remodeled, with additional cabinetry augmenting the pieces already in place, new cabinet fronts can spare the old cabinets from being ripped out and replaced. Simply replace the old cabinet fronts with new ones that are iden-

tical to those of the cabinetry that's part of your addition.

Tip 11 Utility carts offer freestanding storage for the bathroom without the trouble of new construction.

Wearing casters, utility carts are a flexible storage alternative for the bathroom. When you have finished using them, they can be rolled into a deep closet elsewhere in the home, hidden from sight. Or they can be recruited for duty in another room, such as the kitchen.

When new cabinetry is too much expense, or any permanent storage addition such as shelving isn't desired, a utility cart makes sense. It serves your current needs and can be moved with the rest of your household furnishings when you move to a new home.

Tip 12 Consider making pullout wire bins, cabinet-deep drawers, built-in towel racks, and other unusual but highly functional features a part of any custom vanity or cabinetry.

When starting from scratch is an option and you are creating new custom cabinetry in the bathroom, be sure to make the most of your money and effort. A thorough appraisal of your needs will tell you which features your new vanity cabinets should include.

Your style may dictate something less conventional than regular cabinets in the designated cabinet space. Not every inch of your cabinetry has to include drawers or doors. For a different look and function, locker-style wire bins can fit into the space. Or you can leave one lower section of the vanity without cabinetry in order to house towel racks.

SIX

Bedrooms

Bedrooms require a different approach to solving storage needs than other rooms in the home. The reason is simple: more than any other room, the bedroom is intended as a private escape—and its decor should reflect that function with soothing charm. Storage, then, must be addressed in subtle fashion, blending seamlessly with the prevailing mood of the space.

When prospective home buyers are searching for the perfect home, the bedrooms in each potential house inevitably fall under special scrutiny. Even when the sellers would prefer that the bedroom's closet doors remain shut, their own less-than-tidy habits thus kept secret, they know that holding out hope for this seemingly meager vestige of privacy is asking too much. As surely as the sellers will be quizzed about their property taxes, their closet doors will be flung wide open for inspection while quick mental calculations are made: just how much space is available in each bedroom for wardrobes and other personal items that would need to be stored there?

Many an otherwise attractive home is scratched off the list when bedroom storage capacity comes up short. Especially in pre–World War II houses, in which bedroom closets were usually compact, or in older historic houses, in which closets in the sleeping quarters weren't necessarily a standard feature, there must be other compensating features to overcome this handicap. Conversely, some houses that are lacking in character are made much more appealing to the buyer by the simple presence of huge walk-in closets in the bedrooms.

While room-size closets big enough to get lost in are everyone's ideal, they aren't essential for accommodating the wardrobes of any but the most inveterate of clotheshorses. Through planning and organizing, moderate-size closets can be rendered highly functional; their storage capacity can be increased without increasing their actual size. Furthermore, if creative storage solutions are employed, Victorian and historic houses need not be considered obsolete if they lack bedroom closets. Unless the bedrooms in these older houses are especially cramped, storage can be provided by storage-equipped furnishings, portable organizers, and even built-ins that don't detract from the room's architectural integrity, making the lack of closets a moot point.

In terms of decorating, the bedroom requires a unique set of solutions for storage. This is the private space of the home, the intimate retreat sought out as an escape from the demands of daily life. Open storage solutions that worked in the kitchen and bathroom are jarring here, where reminders of daily tasks are not welcome. Serenity, augmented with a little bit of cheer or romance, is most often the mood desired for the bedroom.

Visually, this goal translates into the need for a space in which the eye can travel at ease, with minimal distraction: piles of sweaters or mounds of jeans on the floor, no matter how neatly folded, are aesthetic intruders. See-through tubs stacked on the floor probably aren't much better. The adage "out of sight, out of mind," is best put into practice in these private quarters. Portable storage organizers in full view in the room are reminders of

A wall unit can be added to your closet that is equipped with movable shelves, allowing each shirt or sweater its own "drawer."

Close-Ups on the Closet

Just as improving storage in the bathroom began with a toss-out process, so must it begin in the bedroom closet.

How many times have you worn that red silk blouse in the past year? And the year before? What about those dresses that went out of style years ago? Are you really willing to waste precious closet space while patiently waiting for the fashion tides to turn?

Honestly appraise your wardrobe, then remove everything you haven't worn at least once during the past year. (If you are very resistant to this idea, perhaps you can diminish your throw-away anxiety by not actually removing the no-longer-worn clothing from the home. Storing it in bags or boxes in a less frequently used part of the house is a reasonable compromise that will free up vital bedroom closet space.) With the closet free of all but essential clutter, you can begin appraising its function.

all the complications involved in daily life; however, stashed under the bed, in a cabinet or armoire, or in neat rows in the closet, they are every bit as effective in keeping your space clean and clutter-free.

To plan storage for the bedroom, the best starting point is the closet, for it is here that you will hide a multitude of sins. And it is here that your day will begin on either an orderly, serene note or in a discordant fashion. The choice depends on how well or ill organized your closet may be.

Tip 1   **Organize closets to include space for hanging long items, for double tiers of separates, for folded items, and for shoes.**

The well-designed bedroom closet must include four distinct types of space: space for hanging long items; space for hanging two tiers of separates, one on top of the other; space for folded stacks of clothing; and some sort of space for shoes (though this is one of the most flexible of spatial requirements and doesn't necessarily have to follow any set pattern).

Sometimes home owners are too sloppy not only with how they toss items into the closet, but with how they structure the closet itself. In most closets, the single hanging rod that spans the entire width of the closet has always been there—even though its function is more an impediment than an aid. A single rod for hanging long items could take up half the room that it currently does, with the remaining space better occupied by two tiers of rods, one above the other, for hanging twice the number of separates that were previously accommodated by the old single rod. If your closet doesn't

By installing hanging rods at the narrow ends of a closet, a large space is freed up at the back for mounting racks and pegs for fashion accessories such as headbands, jewelry, sunglasses, and hats.

Old luggage and boxes, with their interesting textures and earthy colors, not only make good storage containers but also add an attractive visual element to the space.

have some type of shelf area, consider adding one. Building a small vertical cabinet doesn't take much skill. Placed in the center of the closet, the shelf area serves as a perfect natural divider for the various compartments of hanging space you need for your clothes.

If you are going to build a cabinet into your closet, consider making it more than a few standard shelves and drawers. Shoe storage space is always at a premium. Why not utilize the space in your new built-in to its greatest advantage with special shoe shelves only inches apart?

Even if you decide not to go to the trouble of building drawers, adding vertical dividing boards to the closet can work as a shell for storing stacked storage boxes and bins and as a divider for different configurations of hanging rods.

If you don't feel up to tackling even the most minimal of building projects, a simple solution for gaining shelf storage space in the closet is to purchase an unfinished (and inexpensive) chest, which you place into the closet just like a built-in. Because this isn't fine furniture, you should have no qualms about screwing rods into its sides or making other adjustments to customize the unit to serve your storage needs.

Men's closets utilize space wisely when they are outfitted with double rods for two rows of hanging clothes, one above the other. When women's wardrobes include a significant number of separates instead of dresses, devoting a portion of the closet to double-hung rows also makes sense.

Space Guides for Planning Your Closet

Keeping a few dimensions in mind is necessary in planning an efficient bedroom closet. The following figures will help you in deciding where to organize your items in a limited closet space.

❑ A standard closet rod for hanging long items should be positioned about 69 inches (175.2cm) above the floor. This will accommodate long dresses and coats, as well as regular dresses and cuff-hung trousers, which take up only about 45 inches (114.3cm) of space.

❑ For smaller separates, including men's and women's suits, double-hung trousers, skirts, blouses, and shirts, use two closet rods hung one above the other. Place the upper rod 76 to 84 inches (193–213.3cm) above the floor. Allow 36 to 42 inches (91.4–106.6cm) from the floor for the lower rod.

❑ Bring each closet rod out from the wall 12 to 14 inches (30.4–35.5cm), for ample space to fit your clothing.

❑ Allow 8 inches (20.3cm) of rod space for every ten blouses or shirts. Allow even more space for bulkier items such as suits.

❑ Add a top shelf to your closet, positioning it about 84 inches (213.3cm) from the floor. This will allow space for a second shelf beneath it, if desired, still above the rods of hanging clothes.

❑ Look to the inside of closet doors as additional potential storage space. If your closet uses bifold or sliding doors, which can't serve as storage, consider replacing them with hinged doors upon which you can mount hooks and racks for such items as shoe bags. Hanging shoe bags require about 36 inches (91.4cm) of vertical space.

❑ On the closet wall space between rods, affix pegs and hooks for hanging belts, ties, and handbags.

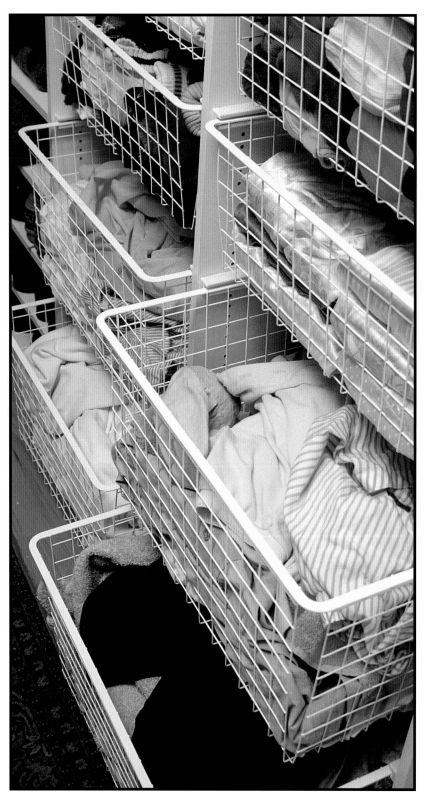

Gone are the days when the bedroom closet meant clothes rods, period. With today's wide range of portable organizers, even the most uninspired closet setup can become a case for efficient space planning, including not only hanging space but an abundance of wire drawers for storage of folded apparel.

Organizers for Everything

The portable organizers that you've enlisted in the kitchen, bath, and other living spaces of your home become not mere conveniences but dear friends in the bedroom, where most of your clothes must be stored. Use them freely, and add to them as you need.

Tip 2 **Purchase portable organizers to meet the specific storage needs of the bedroom: tie racks, shoe bags and boxes, plastic-coated wire bins, cedar stacking boxes for sweaters, hatboxes for fine undergarments, and jewelry containers.**

While many organizers feature a no-nonsense utilitarian look, others are available in softer schemes to fit with a more romantic bedroom theme. Boxes can be found covered in pastel floral paper or fabrics, which lend an air of feminine charm. Before purchasing them, decide whether you will display your organizers behind doors or in the open. If open storage is the answer, look for designer colors even in the more utilitarian units: wire-coated drawers and bins come in a full spectrum of hues.

Tip 3 **Once your closet has been arranged to house your wardrobe efficiently, fill the empty spaces with portable organizers.**

Dead space on the closet floor can be organized to increase storage capacity. Stack boxes, bins, and drawers here, with the most frequently used items on the top. Store those

More and more, closets are becoming design statements as well as storage solutions. Decorative hatboxes in an array of sizes can conceal an assortment of personal items besides hats, while creating an appealing visual vignette as well.

When a closet has been expanded to incorporate a room window, take advantage of the opportunity to create a display space for your most attractive apparel items.

97

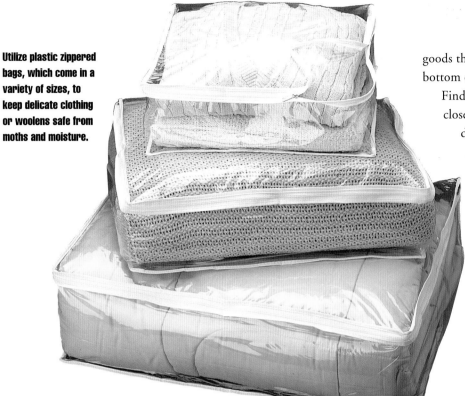

Utilize plastic zippered bags, which come in a variety of sizes, to keep delicate clothing or woolens safe from moths and moisture.

goods that are out of season at the bottom of your stacks.

Find bare wall space inside the closet or on the back of closet doors. Hang tie racks, shoe bags, garment bags, and other necessary organizers here. A tie rack that is only 19 inches (48.2cm) wide can accommodate thirty-four ties, each on its own hook.

Don't forget that hanging plastic wardrobes serve also to protect woolens and delicate clothing. Some people store all their clothes in these zip-up, see-through pouches: the clothes remain lint- and odor-free, as well as carefully organized (suits in one bag, trousers in another, summer dresses in another, and so on).

Outfitted with casters and stacking baskets, the same portable carts that brought ease and organization to the kitchen and bath make great sense in the closet, space permitting. Carts provide instant drawers for folded wardrobe items without the need for constructing a new shelving unit in the closet or purchasing a "real" chest to fit into it. And they can be pulled into the bedroom for greater convenience while dressing.

When a center cabinet isn't present in the closet, use hook-and-grid organizer systems to build storage space from the floor up. Plastic-coated wire shoe racks, for example, can start at the bottom, followed by hook-on shelves for folded goods, handbags, and other various wardrobe accesories.

Wire closet organizers, when properly used, create orderliness from chaos to such a degree that closet doors may not even be necessary.

Entire closet systems, which include wire baskets that can be vertically stacked from the floor to ceiling to contain folded clothing, can be purchased very inexpensively and customized to fit your needs. A typical arrangement might feature two tall stacks of wire baskets at either end of the closet, with a center wire shelf spanning the gap near the ceiling between them. Beneath the center top shelf, a rod for hanging long clothes or two rods for shorter separates can be hooked into the sides of the two stacks of baskets. A special wire rack, slanted on the diagonal for storing shoes, can be hooked into the basket stacks near the floor.

You don't have to spend hundreds of dollars for a workable closet system. For less than thirty dollars, a closet organizer with six adjustable shelves, with widths from 49 to 94 inches (124.4–238.7cm), can be purchased and easily assembled.

Instead of cramming small dressing items such as belts, ties, and soft hats in a dark drawer, add a portable caddy to the closet to arrange the items in easy-to-see, organized fashion.

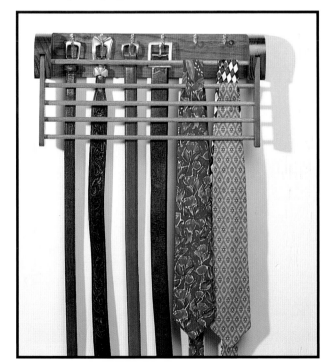

For a spartan bedroom in which even the bed and chairs use minimal lines and suggest a monk's rigor, storage is best addressed within closed doors—with minimal hardware.

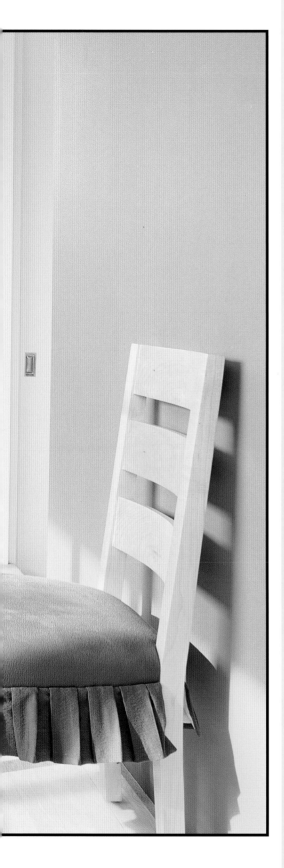

Cupboard Walls: A Different Kind of Closet

In the mid-1960s, a German manufacturer, Interlubke, introduced the first "cupboard wall"—a storage structure that goes beyond its mundane function to actually outfit the room with architecture. A cross between furniture and architecture, these custom units are made to fit the buyer's room dimensions; inside fittings are also customized to accommodate the buyer's personal wardrobe storage needs.

For a bedroom, these walls of cupboards are a new high-end twist on closets. Some, covered in mirrors, create the impression of a larger room while providing all the storage the home owner could want.

Other manufacturers, including Boffi from Italy, have created cupboard wall designs of their own.

The Built-In Bedroom

It's no coincidence that many sleekly efficient bedrooms bring to mind the sleeping quarters of a ship. Even on the finest luxury liners, where the quarters are relatively spacious and elegant, the rooms are designed in streamlined fashion, with everything snugly in place. This is not an aesthetic decision but a practical one: the ship's contents must be secured at all times in the event of rough seas. Thus, closed cabinets with tight-fitting doors are preferred over open storage.

Although wildly strewn items aren't the same kind of issue in the bedrooms of our landlocked homes, we still want to keep stored contents concealed from view. Some of the sweet escapism found on a cruise is due in part to the streamlined setting, which we can choose to emulate in our own homes.

Built-in furnishings for storage are the answer when a sleek environment is the highest priority. More than any other room in the house, the bedroom receives special

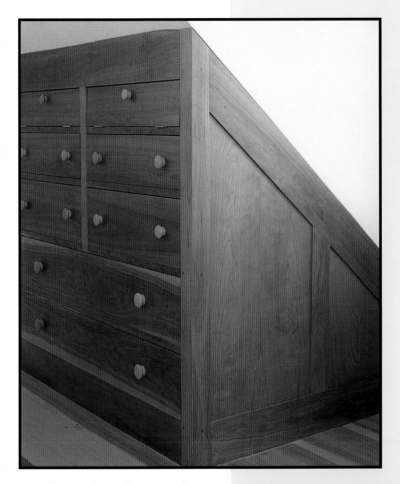

way to create character where none existed before. The most important decision you can make—before any construction begins—is where you want to put your bed. You must make this decision at the beginning of the process, because once the built-ins are created around it, you don't have the luxury of changing your mind.

The bed is the natural starting point for designing a built-in bedroom. It is the largest single furnishing that will be placed in the room, and it is the only one that is absolutely essential. Everything else in the room must flow around it.

In designing your bedroom with storage-efficient built-in features, begin with a diagram of your room with your bed positioned exactly where you want it. Envision one contiguous unit containing the bed, side tables, and shelves, with cabinetry built onto the back of the bed as a headboard, and construction extended out to the sides for built-in bedside tables. With this system, you have no dead space: you no longer need room between the bed and tables, as they are now one sleek unit. You no longer need to provide a visually pleasing space between the headboard and any shelving you might want above it; the shelves, as a built-in part of the bed, are guaranteed their place.

In your new design, extend your efforts to the space beneath the bed, one of the obvious storage spaces of the room. By continuing the wood or laminate finish of your other built-ins to this space, a tidy pullout drawer area for orderly storage can be easily created beneath the bed—without dust bunnies.

consideration for architectural features offering built-in storage. The 1950s and 1960s witnessed a rash of built-in bedroom features in new-home construction. Some of these features have the adverse effect of dating the home. But given a fresh finish—say, with a sponged decorative paint treatment—even these pieces can look up-to-the-minute.

Tip 4 To create a stream-lined bedroom free of visible clutter, add your own architectural built-ins centered around the bed.

When the bedroom is little more than a box, devoid of any architectural embellishment, adding your own built-in storage areas is an excellent

The Best-Kept Secrets

Before lamenting that the dimensions of your bedroom are inadequate for any substantive storage improvements, look to the walls themselves. Perhaps dead space can be transformed into hard-working storage, which can also give the room new architectural importance.

Look to the eaves. If you live in a story-and-a-half, your upstairs bedrooms have some angular oddities at the eaves. Instead of assuming this space is the sacrificial lamb to the home's architecture, reclaim it: the good-for-nothing short, angled spaces can be outfitted as an entire mini-wall of drawers. Also consider bringing out a wall (space permitting) with an entire plane of storage-rich drawers.

By following the perimeter of the room, you can dress the space in as many or as few built-in features as you choose. Entire walls can become sleek closets; other walls can be devoted entirely to closed cabinets, open shelving, or a combination of the two. Desk units which function as computer stations are common built-in features in newer bedrooms (and are especially efficient in a corner location, when they are designed on the diagonal).

Walls that contain windows don't pose a problem in the streamlined bedroom. The flow of built-in features isn't discontinued here, but is merely reinterpreted as a built-in window seat that contains space for storage in the lower section. In the space on either end of the window, the window seat can be surrounded by built-in cabinets or shelves.

Tip 5 **Transform the space beneath the bed into clean, orderly storage by purchasing or making your own drawers and outfitting them with casters.**

The space beneath a bed is often either unutilized or filled with random, unorganized clutter. But you don't have to have a built-in bedroom to have efficient storage beneath the bed. Manufacturers of organizers make particleboard drawers for beneath-the-bed storage. Drawers can be acquired or made to slide under both sides of the bed to fill the entire mattress-size space with efficient storage. Besides allowing additional storage, bed drawers mean an end to vacuuming in this hard-to-reach spot.

Built-in furnishings may be the answer when a sleek environment is a priority in the bedroom.

Kid Stuff

Children's bedrooms are unlike any other room in the home. Though their primary function, like all the other bedrooms, is for sleeping, often that role gets lost in a maze of toys, games, stuffed animals, and books. A kid's room seems more a testament to the human spirit for acquisition—early evidence of the conspicuous consumption that will mark many of the species in later years.

Not only does a child's bedroom contain more "stuff"; it is also constantly evolving at a pace that matches the child's physical, mental, and emotional growth.

Tip 6 Furnish your child's room in modular pieces that have ample storage and room-to-grow potential.

Flexible storage is essential in this room. Whatever storage solutions are found this week may need to be rethought—perhaps disposed of altogether—next week, as the child launches into a new phase.

The best bedroom designs for children are those that are storage-oriented while remaining open-ended, easily added to as the child grows. Often, this translates as modular bedroom components with vast storage comparments.

These pieces can be configured and reconfigured to adapt to changing needs and occasional whims. Shelving units that originally served as homes for a menagerie of stuffed animals, for instance, become receptacles for an expanding library of books and videos as the young child approaches adolescence. Toy-box units give way to desks in this rite of passage. The upper bunk bed may be discarded, with only the lower full-size component used as the

Children's bedrooms, more than the master or guest sleeping quarters, lend themselves especially well to built-ins, which provide ample room to stash toys, stuffed animals, books, and clothes.

teens approach. Shelves that climb the walls as a play tower may continue to serve the growing child's needs for storage—long after the play tower itself has been abandoned.

Tip 7 Unlike an adult's room, a child's bedroom benefits from exposed shelving for colorful open storage that creates visual stimulation.

A major difference between a child's and adult's bedroom is found in the shelving. Closed shelves are prefer-

able for most adults. For kids, the opposite is true. Instead of a calm and soothing haven, kids want visual stimulation—and they should have it—to spark their own mental growth and emotional development.

Instead of concealing everything behind closed cabinet doors, children enjoy having their possessions out in the open. Organization, however, is still essential to this kind of storage; it is important not only for parental peace of mind, but as a valuable lesson in systems and efficiency for the child.

Tip 8 Think about lining your child's room with cabinet-size open shelves as an alternative to standard-size shelves, toy boxes, and case goods.

For relatively little expense, you can transform even a nursery-size child's room into a space with a "place for everything." Cabinet doors are the greatest cost in new cabinetry; when the cabinet spaces are created without the doors, the price tag is only for the particleboard used on the interior structure. With roomy, cabinet-deep

Beds are a prime spot to consider for storage when planning a child's room. Because a child's bed can and possibly should encroach on the realm of fantasy, its configuration can easily be adapted to include toy shelves and hidden drawers.

Create a stage for storage of your child's clothing with a combination drawer-shelf unit you can build yourself using molding as side "walls." Sketching a theatrical drape on wood, then using a jigsaw to cut the design, creates a wooden valence full of dramatic whimsy.

and cabinet-high open shelves tracing the perimeter of the child's bedroom, every toy and stuffed animal is given an orderly home.

Tip 9 **Create top shelves with "loft" play areas that are reached by ladders.**

As long as you are providing ample storage for your child with wraparound tiers of large-size open shelves, make an adventure out of the storage unit. Create a play area above the top shelf that's reached only by ladder. Look at examples from design publications for safety tips. You'll want to include a small safety railing, but be sure its rungs are spaced properly so that no curious child can manage to get his or her head stuck in the safety feature. When the play

loft isn't in use, it can be a form of storage in its own right: a repository for every stuffed animal and toy that didn't manage to land on a shelf below.

Tip 10 **Make visual statements with children's toys: display them on their own, or group them in colorful tubs and baskets.**

Most children's toys can stand on their own as room accessories. Stacks of puzzles piled neatly on top of one another can be in a cache of their own on a deep open shelf. But crayons and colored pencils tend to make a mess unless they are gathered into a container of some sort. Bright tubs in primary colors are excellent receptacles for art supplies and other small play items. Empty coffee tins can also be

used to store small, loose items. Children will appreciate the accessibility of their playthings with an open-storage system, and eventually, they will appreciate the organization, which makes it easy to find the toys they want to play with.

Tip 11 **In a child's room, make good storage use of beneath-the-bed space, perhaps using storage boxes as an affordable alternative to fitted drawers.**

Brightly colored boxes or tubs provide the same organization as drawers for the space under the bed. And, for the ever-changing child's room, these affordable options make better sense than custom-made drawers, which will be antiquated as soon as the bed is outgrown.

109

SEVEN

Special Places

Storage does not have to
be confined to the closets.
This corner space was outfitted with shelves and
stackable organizers to
create an efficient, attractive area to store clothing.
One word of caution: clothing placed near an exposed
window should be pro-
tected because direct sunlight may cause fading.

No matter how effectively you have created storage systems in the main rooms of your home, your household inventory may require even more storage than those spaces permit. Christmas tree ornaments may be your favorite indulgence—but one that the main rooms of the home can't accommodate for out-of-season storage. Or sometimes it makes sense to designate a certain area—a spare bedroom, big closet, garage, attic, or basement room—solely for special storage.

The decision to create special storage spaces is usually because of necessity and availability. When that's the case, storage takes a slightly different approach, utilizing fewer finished furnishings and built-ins in favor of more improvised, make-as-you-go solutions.

The Junk Room

Nearly every home has one: a room tucked away around the corner or up or down the stairs, out of sight, that somehow has become a repository for all the household fallout—everything that couldn't be given a logical place to be stored in another part of the house. This is the room whose doors are always tightly shut. This is the room that guests are routed past. This is the room we're not proud of, yet can't seem to live without.

However great the need for such a catchall space, there's no rule that the room must be an eyesore. It can be a place for wildly different objects we don't know what to do with—but it can also be as strictly organized as military barracks. In this room, imagination must be given free rein if order is to prevail over chaos.

Wall-mounted wire "sleeves" for important papers and transparent plastic boxes on wall-mounted shelves are a good way to organize a work space.

Reinventing Storage Space

A small spare room or a dark, narrow corridor in the basement can be put to new life with a little re-thinking—and hardly any expense.

❏ **Rediscover the power of nails.** Directly hammered into the walls, without cute hangers or decorative mounts, old-fashioned nails prove imminently serviceable for getting clutter off the floor and out of boxes. Tools, baskets, and other paraphernalia too functional to toss find an easy-to-locate home when wall-mounted on nothing more than a bare nail. The walls also gain more of a "room" feel, with functional items artfully arranged in pleasing configurations.

❏ **Enlist old, cast-off bookshelves** or other makeshifts or furniture discards to organize an array of miscellaneous storage goods.

Tip 1 Store appropriate items directly on the wall, hanging them on nails, hooks, or wall-mounted organizers.

Nails boldly hammered into the wall to display handbags, ties, scarves, or jewelry aren't a practical solution for the bedrooms, main living spaces, or even bathrooms of the home. Nails usually require some form of conceal-ment to blend with the interior design of these lived-in spaces, but not so in a special storage room, where the only function of the room is storage.

A folding lattice-work peg board can be adhered to the wall to host small bags, jewelry, and hats.

Trash to Treasure

A junk room is only a junk room when its contents are disorganized. An unfinished room in the basement or attic can be organized with a minimal outlay of cash by using materials on hand.

Investigate using materials already available that are in need of storage. Whether it's leftover lumber from a previous building project or a pair of old doors that you want to hang on to for the future, don't let these items merely occupy space—turn them into storage surfaces for other objects. Lay the doors or lum-ber on top of sawhorses, cinder blocks, or even pails, then organize your surplus cans of paint or miscel-laneous household items on these flat surfaces.

The purpose of a storage room is not high-end design. You don't spend enough time in the room for it to merit the investment of time or money in a full-scale design approach, and no one you want to impress is going to see the room anyway. Although you would never consider makeshift storage solutions like the boards-and-blocks unit discussed above for a real living space in your home, open yourself to the possibility of this working solution for the seldom-visited storage room. There's a strong possibility, too, that once you've improved the organization of the room's clutter through such simple devices, you won't even mind allowing guests a glimpse of the previ-ously off-limits territory. In fact, you may even take pride in your old junk room's new status as an efficiently organized warehouse.

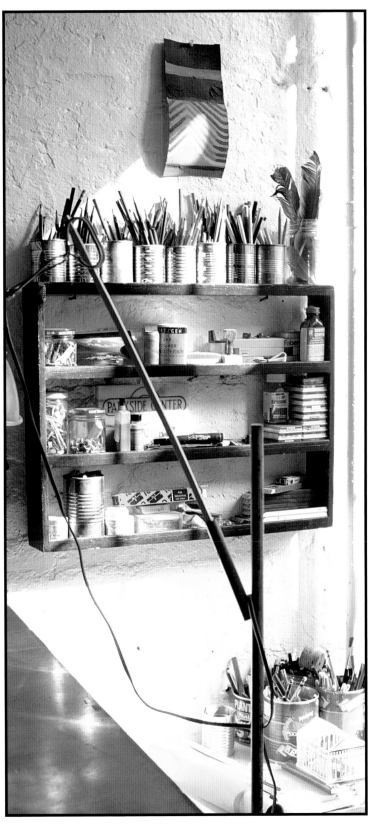

Even primitive wood shelves—freestanding or wall-mounted—can hold artful arrangements of hobby items, from gardening tools and accoutrements to paintbrushes and graphic design aids.

In a storage room, nails driven directly into the wall become handy display areas for a variety of hanging objects—tennis rackets, horse tacks, extra lawn hose, extension cords, spare picture frames, and lawn tools, to name a few. But the nail display shouldn't be shoddily assembled; compose your storage items just as you would any "art," paying attention to balance and scale in your arrangement of items. The result is a room that has to a different set of aesthetic values from that of the home's actual living spaces. Here, a system that provides brisk efficiency and no-nonsense retrieval capabilities provides just the right look—one that comforms with its clear statement of utilitarian intent.

Tip 2 **Create a Christmas storage tree on the wall for an out-of-season display of ornaments.**

Nails hammered in pyramid fashion into a wall create the effect of a Christmas tree. If you're tired of wrapping your ornaments and storing them in boxes between seasons, consider keeping them on display all year long on a wall "tree" in a special storage room.

Tip 3 **Organize the contents of your storage room into room-related sections.**

When it is time to retrieve the lobster pot from the storage room, even a room that appears to be orderly can throw a kink in the day by functioning as something of a Bermuda Triangle. Despite its calm surface appearance, the room has somehow devoured the pot—or whatever else it is you might be searching for.

Focus on Favorites

Golfers, equestrians, tennis players, weekend chefs, fishermen, or others engrossed in a sport may have accumulated a surplus of objects related to their passion. Whether it's ribbons and trophies, photographs, or an abundance of specialized equipment, the spare storage room is an ideal facility for creating an interesting display with them as if they were art or decorative accessories.

Group all the related materials together in one part of the room, which will quickly convey the theme of the display and create a more powerful impact. Utilize wall space, shelves, and the floor. What may seem like kitsch in a living or family room may be warm and endearing in the storage room.

An easy way to get organized and avoid searching for items you need is to arrange household objects in sections related to the rooms in which they typically would be used. The Crock-Pot would be located in the kitchen section of the room, alongside the electric crepe maker and the extra woks that aren't frequently used. The old TV sets, stereos, and records—as well as cutesy room accessories you received from relatives as a gift but can't toss in case they visit—would be organized together in a section that is devoted to family-room goods.

Storage closets don't have to be behind closed doors: they can be exposed areas organized for linens and laundry in tall shelf units, such as seen above.

Collector's Closet

Collectors' homes, though usually among the most interesting, tend to be the most cluttered. The temptation of the collector is to display all the collections at once, for what is loved should be seen. Though collectors know that the impact of their collectibles is diminished when the numbers become too great, few can bear the thought of editing out for storage. The rotation system makes sense, but it also instills panic in a collector.

As a compromise, a closet can be turned into a display of collectibles, arranged with just as much attention and care as those groupings that are presented in the public parts of the home. Even lighting can be customized, with shelves backlit or with pinpoint down lights focusing on specific pieces.

If well designed, the closet can be a visual treat in which the collector delights and even proudly shares with guests and friends. The closet becomes much more than a mere closet; it is an environment composed of objets d'art.

The Storage Closet

Spacious closets in rooms other than the bedroom can serve as halfway houses for out-of-season wardrobes and, thus, can be organized exactly like the bedroom closet (see chapter six). But each extra closet in the home need not be filled with either clothing or household linens. If you have specialized needs, consider turning a closet into a storage receptacle for those objects.

Pegged particleboard answers a range of storage questions in the garage when tacked to walls as a caddy for hammers, tools, and jars easily mounted on pegs inserted into the board. Because no nails have to be hammered into the board, rearrangement of hanging items is as simple as moving pegs. This system, combined with specialized wall mounts for holding larger lawn tools and rows of shelves for cans and jars, turns the messiest garage into an orderly one.

Tip 4 When your home lacks a library and your books seems to outnumber available shelves and bookcases, consider the option of turning a closet into a mini library devoted solely to storing books.

Unless the avid reader's home features a library as part of its floor plan, there's a strong possibility that the home owner's books outnumber shelf or bookcase space. Few book lovers relish the thought of packing away their books in boxes for storage in a spare room, basement, or attic, where moisture or heat can do damage. If there is an extra closet in the home that is not earmarked for some other essential function, consider utilizing it as a book repository. Play with shelf spaces to custom-fit the dimensions of your books, then organize your books according to whatever system you choose (subjects, titles, authors, or even size).

Inexpensive metal shelves, and the floor itself, can be used to organize books for a library effect.

Beyond the Glamour Garage

Some garages are extensions of the home, ornamented with rustic collectibles that make these outdoor spaces as intriguing as their slicker indoor counterparts. But you don't have to have a glamour garage to boast a protected car-park that's a tidy, organized, and extremely functional space for accommodating much more than the family vehicles.

Three walls of the garage are storage opportunities begging for discovery. Woodworkers or weekend handypersons are already well aware of this potential. Work benches that include shelf space for storage can be easily added, wainscoting fashion, to outline the three fixed walls of the garage. Topped with additional tool caddies, wall-mounted shelves, or an arrangement of implements hung directly from nails, these walls afford enough space to organize even the most cumulative collections of outdoor materials and tools.

The Garage

The garage usually must store many other objects besides the family cars within its relatively small confines. Some of the many items that usually must find a home there are lawn tools, bicycles, fishing tackle, toolboxes, and power tools.

Tip 5 To keep the garage's appearance orderly, use the walls for mounting appropriate storage items.

Lawn tools, bikes, fishing gear, bails of wire, and hose can all be mounted on the garage walls, freeing up floor space for the vehicles parked there. Purchase wall-mounted organizers for tools. Group related items together on a wall for quick retrieval. Consider brightening up the space by hanging advertising signs, old posters, memorabilia, or license plates on the walls.

Tip 6 In addition to employing the requisite worktable, organize materials in the garage on small painted benches, which will add a dash of style to the space.

Small painted antique benches are still affordable and don't require great care or maintenance. In other words, you can put them into service in the garage without too much fear of damaging them. Because of their narrow size, they are ideal for snuggling along the sides or front end of the garage. They add color and personality while serving as caddies for small gardening tools, hand tools, or oilcans.

Sources

Mail-Order Companies

Hold Everything
100 North Point Street
San Francisco, CA
94133
(800) 421-2264

Lillian Vernon
510 South Fulton Avenue
Mount Vernon, NY
10550
(800) 285-5555

Tapestry
Hanover House Industries
P.O. Box 46
Hanover, PA
17333-0046
(800) 577-2288

Joan Cook
19 Foster Street
P.O. Box 6038
Peabody, MA
01961
(800) 935-0971

Solutions
P.O. Box 6878
Portland, OR
97228
(800) 342-9988

Companies with Retail Stores Nationwide

The following addresses are the corporate headquarters of the listed companies. Call or write for a store location near you; when available, an 800 number has been listed.

Bed, Bath & Beyond
110 Bicounty Boulevard
Suite 114
Farmingdale, NY
11735
(516) 420-7050

Crate and Barrel
725 Landwehr Road
Northbrook, IL
60062
(800) 323-5461

Ikea North America
B.V. Service Inc.
Plymouth Common
496 Germantown Pike
Plymouth Meeting, PA
19462
(215) 834-0180

California Closets
1700 Montgomery Street
Suite 249
San Francisco, CA
94111
(800) 633-2361

Home Depot
499 Bobby Jones Expressway
Martinez, GA
30907
(706) 650-7662

Index

Photography Credits

©William Abranowicz: pp. *7* middle, 40, 41, 56, *57*, 58 bottom left, 59, 100–101, 119

©Allan Andreson: pp. 44, 45, 68, 85

Courtesy Aristokraft: p. 52 top

Courtesy Brookstone: p. 120 top right and bottom left

©Crandall & Crandall: Design: Viggo Mathiesen: p. *67*

©Daniel Eifert: Design: David Whitcomb, Inc.: p. 35

©Philip Ennis: Design: Connie Beale: pp. 62–63, Design: Blodget Design: p. 21, Design: Ronald Bricke Associates: p. 14, Design: Joyce Dixon Interiors: p. 15 bottom left

©Feliciano: p. 88

©Lois Ellen Frank: Design: Maxine Ordesky (all): pp. 18, 90, 94 top and bottom left, 94–95, 99 top, 106, 119 right

©Michael Garland: Design: Peggy Butcher: p. 15 bottom right, Design: Joe Ruggiero: p. 15 top left, Design: Sherna Steward: pp. 5, 93

©Tria Giovan: pp. 8 bottom, 32, 54–55, *75*, 80 top right and bottom, 81 bottom, 82 bottom, 92, 114 left

©Mick Hales: Architecture: Lee Skolnick: p. 36

©Nancy Hill: pp. 17, 64, 84, 91 (all), 101 middle and bottom right, 112 bottom left, Courtesy Hunter Douglas: 84

©Courtesy Ikea: pp. *7* bottom, 12 top, 26 bottom left, 49 bottom, 52 middle and bottom, 53 right, 58 top left & top and bottom right, 76 (all), 87, 120 top left and bottom right, 121

©Jessie Walker Associates: pp. 38–39, 70–71, *73*, *77*, 107, 114–115

©Lynn Karlin: pp. 20, 112–113

©Tim Lee: pp. 15 top right, 33, 49 middle, 102, 108

©Jennifer Levy: pp. 34, 103, 118

Courtesy Lillian Vernon: pp. *7* top, 8 middle, 12 bottom, 16, 26 top right, 27 (all), 30 bottom, 43 bottom right, 46 (all), 79 top and middle, 80 top left, 81 top and middle, 82 top and middle, 97 top, 98 top, 99 bottom left and right

©Bill Mollet: p. 123

©Michael Mundy: pp. 24, 49 top, 60, 115 right, 121, Design: Mary Rust: p. 19, Design: Stephen Sills: p. 6, Design: Wilkinson: pp. 50–51, Design: Vicente Wolf: p. 74

©Robert Perron: Design: Banks Design Associates: pp. 8 top, 28, Architecture: R.T. Mudge Associates (Courtesy *House Beautiful Homebuilding,* Hearst Corp. © 1994): pp. 65, Architecture: R.T. Mudge Associates: p. 109, Design: Ann Sargent: p. 72, Architecture: Tunney Associates (Courtesy of *House Beautiful Homebuilding,* Hearst Corporation, © 1993): pp. 96, 97 bottom

©David Phelps: pp. 2, 69 (all), 71 top and bottom right, 78, 86, 98 bottom, 116–117

©Eric Roth: pp. 6, 10, 30 top, 42–43, 48, 83, Design: Swan Antiques: p. 25

©Bill Rothschild: pp. 13, 110, Design: Lovelor: p. 22

©Tim Street-Porter: p. 66, Design: Myra Hoefer: p. 29

©Paul Warchol: pp. 104–105